Construction

A Practical Guide to the
RIBA Plan of Work 2013

Stages 4, 5 and 6

Phil Holden

RIBA Publishing

Contents

© RIBA Enterprises, 2015

Published by RIBA Publishing,
66 Portland Place, London, W1B 1AD

ISBN 978 1 85946 572 1

Stock code 83011

The right of Phil Holden to be identified as
the Author of this Work has been asserted in
accordance with the Copyright, Design and Patents
Act 1988, sections 77 and 88.

British Library Cataloguing in Publications Data
A catalogue record for this book is available from
the British Library.

Commissioning editor: Sarah Busby
Production: Michèle Woodger
Designed and typeset by: Alex Lazarou
Printed and bound by: CPI
Cover image: © iStock/ewg3D

While every effort has been made to check the
accuracy and quality of the information given in this
publication, neither the Author nor the Publisher
accept any responsibility for the subsequent use of
this information, for any errors or omissions that it
may contain, or for any misunderstandings arising
from it.

RIBA Publishing is part of RIBA Enterprises Ltd.
www.ribaenterprises.com

Foreword

This comprehensive, step-by-step guide charts a very thorough path through what can be a difficult process at times. It presents an accurate and detailed approach, for both architects and all construction professionals throughout the industry, as to the best practice in the delivery of the final phases of the RIBA Plan of Work 2013.The author's unique experience in the design and construction of projects of varying complexity worldwide, allied with his technical expertise, provides an invaluable insight into the industry regarding the processes and techniques adopted in the successful delivery of construction projects. It is an informative read and provides an easy to follow structure to the primary activities, roles and responsibilities of the architect and their interface with the wider design team, captured within a range of procurement methodologies. The illustration of these design and construction processes within a variety of development scenarios, from a small residential extension to a new office headquarters, provides an easily identifiable framework for all. A great benchmark to which we can all aspire.

Richard Paul
Partner, Rogers Stirk Harbour + Partners LLP

Series editor's foreword

The RIBA Plan of Work Stage Guides are a crucial accompaniment to the RIBA Plan of Work 2013. The plan's format cannot communicate or convey the detail behind every term in the plan and this series provides essential guidance by considering, in depth, the reasoning and detail behind many new and reinvigorated subjects linking these to practical examples. The series is comprised of three titles which each concentrate on distinct stages in the Plan of Work. The first is Briefing by Paul Fletcher and Hilary Satchwell which covers Stages 7, 0 and 1. The second is Design by Tim Bailey and this covers Stages 2 and 3. The third is Construction by Phil Holden and covers Stages 4, 5 and 6. Subjects explored include how to assemble the most appropriate and effective project team and how to develop the best possible brief. The series also considers how to deal with the cultural shifts arising from a shift from "analogue" to transformational "digital" design processes as our industry begins to absorb the disruptive technologies that are changing many different and diverse sectors beyond recognition.

The RIBA Plan of Work 2013 drives a shift towards richer and bigger data which can be harnessed to create better whole life outcomes and thus significant additional benefits to clients and users. The first book in the series, Briefing, considers how the new project stages (0 and 7) will add value over the lifetime of a project as greater emphasis is placed on more resilient designs where whole life considerations are embedded into the early design stages. With this in mind the series emphatically starts with Stage 7 placing emphasis on the importance of learning from previous projects via feedback and in the future via data analytics. This initial chapter also sets out how post occupancy and building performance evaluations can be harnessed to inform the Business Case during Stage 0 underlining that big data will provide paradigm shifts in how to extract feedback from newly completed or existing projects, including historic buildings, to help better decision making in the early project stages.

More specifically, Paul and Hilary's book considers new Stage 7 to 0 activities that will result in exciting new services in the future. These will ensure that the client's brief is robust and properly considered providing the best possible platform for the design stages. This publication also considers the importance of site appraisals at Stage 0 and how Feasibility Studies can assist and add value at Stage 1 to the briefing process before the design process commences in earnest at Stage 2. In every stage there is added emphasis around Information Exchanges and the importance of considering who does what when at the outset of a project.

Although the core design stages (2 and 3) have not significantly changed, Tim Bailey's book, Design, looks at how they might be adjusted and better focused to provide greater client emphasis at Stage 2 allowing the lead designer to take centre stage at Stage 3. During this stage greater emphasis is placed on the production of a co-ordinated design: the design team should be focused on the work required to verify that the Concept Design is robust and suitable for making a Planning application. In both stages new methods of communicating the progressing design create exciting new opportunities but at the same time require an examination of how to effectively manage the design process using tools such as the Design Programme to manage what is an iterative process.

Finally, Phil Holden's book, Construction, considers the complexities of Stage 4 which is "sliced and diced" in different ways depending on the procurement route and the extent of design work undertaken by the specialist subcontractors employed by the contractor. He considers how the Design Programme for this change might alter to reflect different procurement routes and how this stage typically overlaps with construction (Stage 5). Handing over projects is becoming increasing complex and users now realise that the handover process can impact on successful operation and use of their buildings. Phil considers how the handover process is changing, placing greater emphasis on the user's needs. His Stage 6 narrative considers how building contracts might adapt to this new environment placing greater emphasis on whole life matters including achieving better project outcomes rather than focusing on the closure solely of contractual matters and construction defects.

Five project scenarios weave through the series providing some practical examples of how the different stages of the plan of work might be interpreted on projects of differing scales, sectors, complexity using different procurement routes, providing a consistent thread through all of the books.

In summary, the series provides excellent additional guidance on how to use the RIBA Plan of Work 2013 allowing anyone involved in the built environment to understand and use the plan more effectively with the goal of achieving better whole life outcomes.

The author

Phil Holden recently retired after 15 years as Managing Director of Pascall+Watson Ltd, an internationally renowned firm of architects with offices in Ireland, Abu Dhabi and Qatar. Phil has spent over thirty years in practice working on a variety of complex projects at both the design and delivery stages. For the last ten years he has led this AJ100 practice to prominence working on an international portfolio of major projects. He is an accomplished designer and an expert in framework relationship and supply chain management gained from years of experience with clients across the transportation, education and commercial sectors. Through the completion of many major projects he has gained an in-depth experience of the techniques required to run and deliver significant architectural projects. This has resulted in Phil being instrumental in developing the BIM overlay to the Plan of Work and working on the development of the RIBA Plan of Work 2013.

Acknowledgements

The author would like to thank Pascall + Watson architects for the experience and support they have provided throughout the development of this book. I would also like to thank Tony Ward, Martin Neilan and Steve West for their contribution to some of the sketches and diagrams, Hugo Camacho of Martifer who assisted in the provision of typical supplier documentation at Stage 4, Dale Sinclair, the series editor, for the clarity he provided on the earlier drafts and Sarah Busby for her patience, guidance and support in bringing the book to conclusion. Writing this book has enabled me to create a reference document for the collaborative team, architects and students of architecture who are keen to understand the practical application of Stages 4, 5 and 6 of the RIBA Plan of Work 2013. It could not have been achieved without the experience provided through over 30 years designing and delivering highly complex collaborative projects, the inspiration provided by my son Aaron, as he completed his architectural training, the enthusiasm provided from my daughter Fenella and the understanding and lifelong support of my wife Beverley.

The series editor

Dale Sinclair is Director of Technical Practice for AECOM's architecture team in EMEA. He is an architect and was previously a Director of Dyer and an Associate Director at BDP. He has taught at Aberdeen University and the Mackintosh School of Architecture and regularly lectures on BIM, design management and the RIBA Plan of Work 2013. He is passionate about developing new design processes that can harness digital technologies, manage the iterative design process and improve design outcomes.

He is currently the RIBA Vice President, Practice and Profession, a trustee of the RIBA Board, a UK board member of BuildingSMART and a member of various Construction Industry Council working groups. He was the editor of the BIM Overlay to the Outline Plan of Work 2007, edited the RIBA Plan of Work 2013 and was author of its supporting tools and guidance publications: Guide to Using the RIBA Plan of Work 2013 and Assembling the Collaborative Project Team.

The scenarios

Throughout the series five projects of different scale, sector and complexity have been used to illustrate the practical impact of the RIBA Plan of Work 2013. These look at how different projects may need to deal differently with a range of issues that could arise. These are not intended to be definitive examples of what to do, or what not to do, but to aid understanding of the plan of work and how different approaches may be adopted at each stage to support better project outcomes. They are:

- **Scenario A: An extension to a four-bedroom house in a rural location.** This project is for a private client and has a budget of £250k. The design team have been selected by recommendation from friends and are appointed to help the client develop the brief. The chosen procurement route is the traditional procurement of a contractor by the client.
- **Scenario B: A small scale housing development for a local developer on the outskirts of a large city.** The value of the project is £1.5million and the client is a small but well established family business. Both the design team and the contractor are to be selected by informal tender with previous experience and pricing core evaluation factors. The procurement route is also traditional.
- **Scenario C: The refurbishment of a teaching building for a University which has a large portfolio of buildings.** The value of the project is between £5million – £6million. The design team are selected following a mini competition. The procurement route is single stage design and build with the design team being novated to the contractor.
- **Scenario D: A new central library for a medium sized Local Authority.** Following the development of the brief including Feasibility Studies produced by a directly appointed team on the Council's Consultant Framework the project is tendered to select the design team for the next stages. The contractor is to be selected following a two stage design and build process and will appoint their own design team. The original design team is to be retained by the council as advisors.
- **Scenario E: A large office scheme for a high tech internet based company wanting to establish themselves as major players in the industry with a high profile new base.** Valued at £18 million - £20 million this project is procured using a management form of contract due to the urgent need to occupy the building.

At the end of each Stage in the book there is a status check on the five projects where the impact of the work and decisions made during that stage are illustrated. Within each chapter these scenarios are used to identify key points and examples.

The in-text boxed features

We have also included several in-text boxed features to enhance your understanding of the Plan of Work stages and their practical application.

The following key will explain what each icon means and why each feature is useful to you:

 The 'Example' feature explores an example from practice, either real or theoretical, and often utilizing the project scenarios.

 The 'Hints and Tips' feature dispenses pragmatic advice and highlights common problems and solutions.

 The 'Definition' feature explains key terms in more detail.

RIBA ♔

RIBA Plan of Work 2013

The **RIBA Plan of Work 2013** organises the process of briefing, designing, constructing, maintaining, operating and using building projects into a number of key stages. The content of stages may vary or overlap to suit specific project requirements.

Tasks ▼	**0** Strategic Definition	**1** Preparation and Brief	**2** Concept Design	**3** Developed Design
Core Objectives	Identify client's **Business Case** and **Strategic Brief** and other core project requirements.	Develop **Project Objectives**, including **Quality Objectives** and **Project Outcomes**, **Sustainability Aspirations**, **Project Budget**, other parameters or constraints and develop **Initial Project Brief**. Undertake **Feasibility Studies** and review of **Site Information**.	Prepare **Concept Design**, including outline proposals for structural design, building services systems, outline specifications and preliminary **Cost Information** along with relevant **Project Strategies** in accordance with **Design Programme**. Agree alterations to brief and issue **Final Project Brief**.	Prepare **Developed Design**, including coordinated and updated proposals for structural design, building services systems, outline specifications, **Cost Information** and **Project Strategies** in accordance with **Design Programme**.
Procurement *Variable task bar	Initial considerations for assembling the project team.	Prepare **Project Roles Table** and **Contractual Tree** and continue assembling the project team.	◁- The procurement strategy does not fundamentally alter the progression of the design or the level of detail prepared at	a given stage. However, **Information Exchanges** will vary depending on the selected procurement route and **Building Contract**. A bespoke **RIBA Plan of Work**
Programme *Variable task bar	Establish **Project Programme**.	Review **Project Programme**.	Review **Project Programme**.	◁- The procurement route may dictate the **Project Programme** and result in certain stages overlapping
(Town) Planning *Variable task bar	Pre-application discussions.	Pre-application discussions.	◁- Planning applications are typically made using the Stage 3 output.	A bespoke **RIBA Plan of Work 2013** will identify when the
Suggested Key Support Tasks	Review **Feedback** from previous projects.	Prepare **Handover Strategy** and **Risk Assessments**. Agree **Schedule of Services**, **Design Responsibility Matrix** and **Information Exchanges** and prepare **Project Execution Plan** including **Technology** and **Communication Strategies** and consideration of **Common Standards** to be used.	Prepare **Sustainability Strategy, Maintenance and Operational Strategy** and review **Handover Strategy** and **Risk Assessments**. Undertake third party consultations as required and any **Research and Development** aspects. Review and update **Project Execution Plan**. Consider **Construction Strategy**, including offsite fabrication, and develop **Health and Safety Strategy**.	Review and update **Sustainability, Maintenance and Operational** and **Handover Strategies** and **Risk Assessments**. Undertake third party consultations as required and conclude **Research and Development** aspects. Review and update **Project Execution Plan**, including **Change Control Procedures**. Review and update **Construction** and **Health and Safety Strategies**.
Sustainability Checkpoints	**Sustainability Checkpoint — 0**	**Sustainability Checkpoint — 1**	**Sustainability Checkpoint — 2**	**Sustainability Checkpoint — 3**
Information Exchanges (at stage completion)	**Strategic Brief.**	**Initial Project Brief.**	**Concept Design** including outline structural and building services design, associated **Project Strategies**, preliminary **Cost Information** and **Final Project Brief**.	**Developed Design**, including the coordinated architectural, structural and building services design and updated **Cost Information**.
UK Government Information Exchanges	Not required.	Required.	Required.	Required.

*Variable task bar – in creating a bespoke project or practice specific RIBA Plan of Work 2013 via www.ribaplanofwork.com a specific bar is selected from a number of options.

The **RIBA Plan of Work 2013** should be used solely as guidance for the preparation of detailed professional services contracts and building contracts.

www.ribaplanofwork.com

4 ⟳ Technical Design	5 ⟳ Construction	6 ⟳ Handover and Close Out	7 ⟳ In Use
Prepare **Technical Design** in accordance with **Design Responsibility Matrix** and **Project Strategies** to include all architectural, structural and building services information, specialist subcontractor design and specifications, in accordance with **Design Programme**.	Offsite manufacturing and onsite **Construction** in accordance with **Construction Programme** and resolution of **Design Queries** from site as they arise.	Handover of building and conclusion of **Building Contract**.	Undertake **In Use** services in accordance with **Schedule of Services**.
2013 will set out the specific tendering and procurement activities that will occur at each stage in relation to the chosen procurement route. ➜	Administration of **Building Contract**, including regular site inspections and review of progress.	Conclude administration of **Building Contract**.	
or being undertaken concurrently. A bespoke **RIBA Plan of Work 2013** will clarify the stage overlaps.	The **Project Programme** will set out the specific stage dates and detailed programme durations. ➜		
planning application is to be made. ➜			
Review and update **Sustainability, Maintenance and Operational** and **Handover Strategies** and **Risk Assessments**. Prepare and submit Building Regulations submission and any other third party submissions requiring consent. Review and update **Project Execution Plan**. Review **Construction Strategy**, including sequencing, and update **Health and Safety Strategy**.	Review and update **Sustainability Strategy** and implement **Handover Strategy**, including agreement of information required for commissioning, training, handover, asset management, future monitoring and maintenance and ongoing compilation of '**As-constructed' Information**. Update **Construction** and **Health and Safety Strategies**.	Carry out activities listed in **Handover Strategy** including **Feedback** for use during the future life of the building or on future projects. Updating of **Project Information** as required.	Conclude activities listed in **Handover Strategy** including **Post-occupancy Evaluation**, review of **Project Performance, Project Outcomes** and **Research and Development** aspects. Updating of **Project Information**, as required, in response to ongoing client **Feedback** until the end of the building's life.
Sustainability Checkpoint — 4	**Sustainability Checkpoint — 5**	**Sustainability Checkpoint — 6**	**Sustainability Checkpoint — 7**
Completed **Technical Design** of the project.	'**As-constructed' Information**.	Updated '**As-constructed' Information**.	'**As-constructed' Information** updated in response to ongoing client **Feedback** and maintenance or operational developments.
Not required.	Not required.	Required.	As required.

© RIBA

Introduction

The RIBA Plan of Work 2013

Building a solid reputation for delivery is as important to any architectural practice as being renowned for its design skills. Mies van der Rohe stated, 'God is in the details', and if conceptual designers lose their relationship with the art of detailing and seeing how things are built, then the concepts prepared by them will become uninformed, flawed and difficult to construct. The RIBA Plan of Work 2013 provides a continuous framework for the design, development, detailing and delivery of a project. Stage 4 Technical Design, Stage 5 Construction and Stage 6 Handover and Close Out are particularly associated with the delivery of a building. This guide starts by illustrating how a successful outcome for Stage 4 Technical Design is predicated on the quality of the information produced at Stage 3 Developed Design. This consistent requirement for high-quality information is repeated at each of the Information Exchange points between the stages.

Introducing the Stage Guides

This book is the third in a series of guides for architects to the RIBA Plan of Work 2013. The first book in the series – Briefing: A Practical Guide to the RIBA Plan of Work 2013 Stages 7, 0 and 1 – deals with the continuous cycle found in building projects. As buildings are put into use, information can be gathered, disseminated and analysed at Stage 7 before being used to inform the briefing process for future projects at Stages 0 and 1. The second book in the series, Design: A practical guide to RIBA Plan of Work 2013 Stages 2 and 3, describes the development of a project from the brief, into Concept Design and through Developed Design. It establishes the content of many of the project strategies and tools that are required to develop a building design. This, the third book in the series, commences at the end of Stage 3 once the design has been coordinated. It describes how to turn the design information into a Technical Design that will enable the project to be constructed. It deals with the role of the design team during construction and what happens at Stage 6 when the building is handed over.

What is this book about?

Transforming an exciting design concept into a building that delivers all of the outcomes envisaged for a project takes a great deal of experience and a wealth of technical expertise, and demands the highest level of collaborative

Stage	7 In Use	0 Strategic Definition	1 Preparation and Brief	2 Concept Design	3 Developed Design	4 Technical Design	5 Construction	6 Handover & Close Out	7 In Use
Review/ analysis	Book 1: Briefing — In Use Data, Strategic Brief, Concept Design								
Design/ synthesis			Book 2: Design — Final Project Brief, Developed Design						
Delivery/ process						Book 3: Construction — Technical Design, Construction, Handover			

0.1

Each book in the Stage Guides series mapped against RIBA Plan of Work 2013.

behaviour from the project team. Stages 4, 5 and 6 of the RIBA Plan of Work 2013 provide a framework to support the project team in developing the Technical Design, completing the construction and handover of the building to the client. It is the point at which the contractor and the specialist subcontractors become fully engaged with the project. The project lead and the lead designer must ensure, as the team grows, that they have conveyed the vision for the building. It is the time when a Developed Design is turned into Technical Design information that will enable the project to be built.

To achieve a successful start to Stage 4 Technical Design, it is important to understand the status of the project at the end of Stage 3 Developed Design. Many of the strategic decisions will have already been made by the project team, namely:

- What is the chosen procurement strategy?
- What is the overall time available for the project programme?
- How much has been allowed for in the project budget?
- Who are the key members of the project team?

Stages 4, 5 and 6 under the microscope

What to expect in the Information Exchange at the end of Stage 3 and how to review the status of the project will be considered in Chapter 1. The transition from Stage 3 to Stage 4 is key to a successful construction stage; the design should already be coordinated in order to avoid unnecessary work in Stage 4. Chapter 1 will describe what needs to be in place before Stage 4 should be commenced.

Chapter 2 explains how to get started on the Stage 4 Technical Design. It will describe what level of information needs to be provided at this stage, how to develop the Design Responsibility Matrix created at Stage 1 and how to develop a Design Programme for this stage. Many of the decisions taken during Stage 4 are affected by the procurement route selected at Stages 2 or 3 or even earlier, and within this chapter there is an explanation of how this selection affects Stage 4.

In order to complete Stage 4 the project team will need to undertake a number of key support tasks, and these are described in Chapter 3. This chapter covers how to update the strategies developed in the earlier stages for health and safety, maintenance, operation and handover together with the Sustainability Strategy. The chapter also describes the outstanding approvals that may be required, how to ensure that the project details are complete and how to undertake a value-engineering exercise if this is required.

Having completed Technical Design at Stage 4, the next stage deals with the construction of the building. At Stage 5 the responsibility for the project is handed to the contractor, with the rest of the project team there to ensure that they have all of the information required to complete the building in accordance with the Construction Programme. Stage 5 will include all the activities to be completed on site as well as any of the off-site manufacture of components that have been designed for the building. Chapter 4 will describe how to prepare for this stage – in particular, dealing with contractor mobilisation, what to do if you are appointed as contract administrator, how to deal with design queries from site, how to prepare for a site inspection and how to approach the processes required throughout the construction phase of the project. It will describe how to prepare for the Information Exchange at the end of Stage 5, including what to include in the 'As-constructed' Information. It will touch briefly on what is required to complete the building, and how to prepare for handover and occupation.

Unlike other stages, the commencement of Stage 6 Handover and Close Out is not predicated on the completion of Stage 5 Construction. It is a stage that must be started some time before practical completion is reached in order that the services installation can be adequately commissioned, the project team have sufficient time to ensure that the appropriate quality is reached and the documentation can be prepared for the completion of the project. Chapter 5 will describe the activities to be completed leading up to handover. It will highlight the responsibilities of different members of the project team at this stage. What happens at handover will be referred to, and there will be a description of the post-occupancy evaluation services that may be commissioned by the client to monitor the building during Stage 7 In Use. In addition, the project team need to induct the client and/ or owner of the building into the way in which it is designed to work, and this is conveyed in the form of a User Guide to the building. Finally, there will be a description of the activities to be completed in order for the client to gain occupation.

CHAPTER 01

STARTING STAGES 4, 5 AND 6

OVERVIEW

This chapter provides an overview of the core objectives at Stages 4, 5 and 6 and how they impact on the project team. It will describe how far the design should have progressed by the end of Stage 3 Developed Design, and what information is required in order to achieve a successful start to Stage 4 Technical Design. It will detail what to expect with regard to the Cost Information at the end of Stage 3, and what the status of planning permission should be at this stage. Finally, it will review what the design team should expect to receive in the Information Exchange at the end of Stage 3, and provide a summary of where our sample projects should be.

WHAT IS IN THE EIGHT TASK BARS
at Stages 4, 5 and 6?

Under each stage, there are eight task bars describing the key activities that need to be completed in order for the project to progress through that stage.

Task Bar 1: Core Objectives

In this task bar the core objectives and the principal activities for each stage are set out. At Stage 4 it refers to the preparation of Technical Design in accordance with the Design Responsibility Matrix (DRM) and the already established Project Strategies. Once all the specialist subcontractors are appointed the DRM can be checked and updated if necessary. At this stage reference is also made to completing the Technical Design, including all the work of the specialist subcontractors in accordance with a Design Programme. The core objectives of Stage 5 include the resolution of any Design Queries and the construction of the project in accordance with the Construction Programme. At Stage 6 the core objectives are to hand over the building and complete the Building Contract.

Task Bar 2: Procurement

The RIBA Plan of Work 2013 has a pull-down list of alternative procurement choices, which contributes to the creation of a bespoke Plan for each project. The options available are:

- Traditional contract.
- Single-stage design and build contract (with Employer's Requirements defined at Stage 3).
- Two-stage design and build contract (with Employer's Requirements defined at Stage 4).
- Management contract.
- Contractor-led contract.

The decision on the preferred procurement route may be taken at the very outset of the project, but should be determined no later than Stage 2. If the chosen procurement route is single- or two-stage design and build, some of Stage 4 may be incorporated in the Contractor's Proposals. If the chosen procurement route is traditional, then Stage 4 Technical Design information will need to be complete before the project is tendered. In Chapter 2, there is a description of how to deal with tender action for this method of procurement.

Task Bar 3: Programme

The stages of the RIBA Plan of Work 2013 are generally sequential, and follow the progression of a project from commencement to completion and beyond. The Project Programme, established at the start of the project, describes the duration of each stage and in general terms should not require updating at Stage 4. In some instances the stages may not be sequential – but rather, Stages 4 and 5 may overlap. This is particularly prevalent in management contracts, in which the work is often tendered in packages. Within a bespoke RIBA Plan of Work 2013 the Project Programme option is determined by the procurement route selected, reflecting the fact that procurement fundamentally frames the Project Programme and that stages might overlap.

Task Bar 4: Town Planning

When to submit for planning is a further option in enabling the customisation of the RIBA Plan of Work 2013. This can occur during Stage 2 or Stage 3 (the latter being the recommended stage). During Stages 4 and 5 the only planning matters to be dealt with will include discharging the specific conditions attached to the planning approval. On most projects it would be unusual for Stage 4 to commence before planning permission is obtained.

Task Bar 5: Suggested Key Support Tasks

This task bar describes the key support tasks that are required at each stage. During Stages 4 and 5 one of the main support tasks is to review and update all the project strategy documents. This ensures that buildability, health and safety, maintenance, operation, sustainability and handover are all considered. In addition, at Stage 4 all the remaining approvals are to be obtained, such as that for Building Regulations. At Stage 6 the project team carry out the activities listed in the Handover Strategy.

Task Bar 6: Sustainability Checkpoints

The sustainability checkpoints ensure that the project is developed in a sustainable way. At Stage 4 the team prepare the Building Regulations Part L submission, together with the future climate impact assessment once all the systems and operating protocols are established. Details are audited for airtightness and continuity of insulation. In addition, the maintenance team should be consulted on the environmental control systems to be adopted.

Task Bar 7: Information Exchanges

Although each project may have different requirements on the type of information to be included in the Information Exchange, knowing what the expected deliverable is will ensure a successful outcome to the stage. This task bar provides guidance on the type of information to be included.

Task Bar 8: UK Government Information Exchanges

This is a specific task bar for government projects. It recognises that, as a client, government does not need to be involved in all Information Exchanges. Specifically with regard to this guide, once a government client has received and approved the information at the end of Stage 3, they do not require further information until the project is ready for handover.[1]

[1] Guide to Using the RIBA Plan of Work 2013, RIBA.

WHAT ARE THE CORE OBJECTIVES
of Stages 4, 5 and 6?

By the time Stage 4 in the RIBA Plan of Work 2013 is started, all the major design decisions will have been made and the relationship between many of the different building components will be fixed. The design will be coordinated and aligned with the Project Budget. The core objective of Stage 4 is to turn the Developed Design into a comprehensive set of Technical Design information that will enable the contractor to undertake construction. The information can also be used to form the basis of information for the handover of the building and to facilitate the operation of the building. This information is completed by the design team and supplemented by the Technical Design information prepared by the specialist subcontractors. The lead designer has a major role to play during Stage 4. As the project team grows in size there are more detailed interfaces to coordinate, and the work of the specialist subcontractors needs to be integrated into the design information. The project lead will need to ensure

USING THE DESIGN RESPONSIBILITY MATRIX AT STAGE 4

The DRM will be completed at Stage 1. It will define the interfaces between areas of work and clearly establish who is responsible for each area. The design team will base their fee on this schedule of responsibility, making sure that their role is defined and priced correctly. An early engagement with the contractor may have an impact on the DRM prepared by the design team. The contractor may prefer to procure certain packages from suppliers who do not have an in-house design capability and who may turn to the design team to complete the design. In these circumstances the design team will be able to use the DRM to establish with the contractor that this additional scope will demand further fees, or a reduction.

that this specialist input is available at the right time, and completing the Design Responsibility Matrix at Stage 1 will ensure that this happens. The Design Programme, started at Stage 2, will be updated to reflect the level of detail to be produced at this stage. The Design Responsibility Matrix, developed at Stage 1, may also be updated at the commencement of Stage 4, and this will be utilised to ensure that everyone understands their role in the team.

By the time Stage 5 Construction is reached, the work of the Design Team will be complete. This is the culmination of the design stages, and the lead designer will pass on the responsibility for the Project Information to the contractor. During this stage the design team will continue to answer any Design Queries from the contractor. These will arise because, despite advances in design software ensuring that design information is coordinated at the end of Stage 3 and integrated at the end of Stage 4, it may require interpretation should unknown site conditions be encountered. In addition to answering Design Queries, the design team may be engaged to inspect the works. The benefit of the original designers undertaking inspection responsibilities is that it will enable them to ensure that the required quality is reached as well as anticipating potential problems. However, if novated to the contractor under a design and build contract this is not usually the case.

The contractor or client may use Stage 5 to ensure that the role of those responsible for inspections is comprehensive and covers the inspection of any work off as well as on site. This may involve the design team visiting manufacturers in remote areas, but it will pay dividends when products arrive on site with no defects.

Before Stage 5 is complete the construction lead will instigate the handover process associated with Stage 6 Handover and Close Out. This will start before construction completes, as equipment must be commissioned and any defective workmanship corrected prior to handover. With Practical Completion the contractor will pass on the building, the 'As-constructed' Information and the user guide to the client. At this stage the client takes control of the building and prepares for occupation (part of Stage 6) and Stage 7 In Use.

HOW FAR SHOULD THE DESIGN HAVE
progressed by the time Stage 4 is reached?

The RIBA plan of Work 2013 prescribes that by the time the end of Stage 3 is reached the design will be coordinated, the Concept Design validated and a number of key decisions will have been made. It would be appropriate to expect that the key aspects of the project are defined, that the rules for the integration of the design are established and that all elements that are fundamental to the predictability of cost, construction and operation are fixed. To develop a truly coordinated design it is necessary to progress the mechanical and electrical design from the diagrams of intent, often produced by engineers at Stage 3, into information showing sizes and locations of all but the most minor pieces of equipment. The designers will also have considered all safety issues that may arise during the construction, maintenance, operation and demolition of the project. Any permanent mitigation solutions will be embedded in the design for the project.

The information available from the design team at the end of Stage 3 should include either drawings that enable the project team to understand the layout of the building, the systems (such as those for cladding, walls and ceilings) that form the building and the major components within them, or a Level 2 Building Information Model conveying the same information.

LEVEL 2 BUILDING INFORMATION MODEL (BIM)

Level 2 BIM requires the production of 3D information models by all key members of the collaborative project team. The final model will be formed of separate models prepared by individual disciplines (architectural, structural and mechanical). The lead designer will provide comments on all models to ensure that the information being presented is robust. By the end of Stage 3 these individual models will be combined into a federated model in a common data environment.

The level of design information should include the following:

- Architectural layouts.
- Architectural elevations and sections or a Level 2 BIM coordinated model.
- Typical details of important or complex interfaces.
- Fire compartmentation.
- Mechanical layout plans (not just schematics).
- Electrical layout plans, including information on specialist systems.
- Phasing drawings.
- Elemental cost plan.

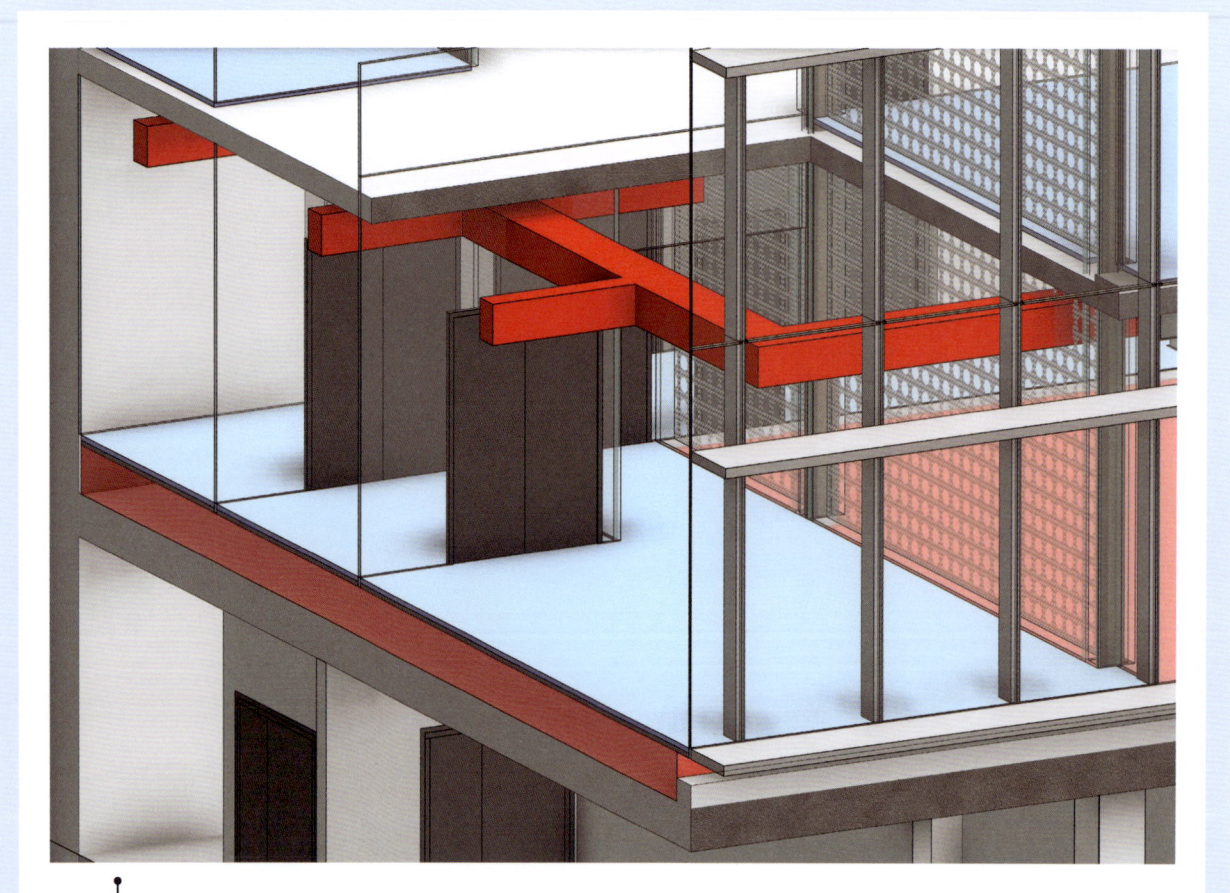

1.1
Illustration showing how all the systems and components come together at Stage 3.

The illustration at Figure 1.1 shows that:

- Structural size and locations have been fixed.
- Zones have been established for underfloor services and for exposed ductwork at high level (marked in red).
- Elevations have been resolved and solar shading has been incorporated as a design intent.
- All the major architectural components – walls, raised floors, etc. – have been defined in the model.

What to expect in the Cost Information at the end of Stage 3

As part of the briefing process at Stage 1, a Project Budget will be set. As the design progresses through Concept Design and Developed Design, the design team will produce a design that meets the Project Budget. To help them achieve this, the cost consultant will prepare regular construction cost estimates. At the end of each stage the latest construction cost estimate will be reconciled with the Project Information and signed off by the client. By the time the project reaches the end of Stage 3 the design will be fully coordinated and a great deal will be known about the materials and finishes chosen. The construction cost estimate should now have changed from a square-metre calculation used at the outset of the project, to an elemental cost plan.

ELEMENTAL COST PLAN

An elemental cost plan gives the individual costs for all the major components of a building – eg walls, floor, ceilings. It enables the design team to design to cost, and enables the cost consultant to identify those items that appear expensive when compared to elemental cost plans of other similar buildings. It ensures that the design team and the client focus on areas where savings can be achieved. As Building Information Modelling progresses into Level 3 it will be possible for the design team to reference similar building cost plans and interrogate their own building model to keep the project on budget.

It is important that the cost consultant uses his of her experience to develop a realistic cost for the building, as not all the detail will be illustrated in the Project Information at this stage. In addition, a contingency figure should be included within the estimate. In general, it is practical to assume that the building cost estimate at this stage is within 10% of the final cost.

WHOLE-LIFE COSTS

Whole-life costing is a means of comparing options and their associated cost over a period of time. Costs to be taken into account include both initial ones such as design, construction and installation costs and future ones such as operating costs, rent, rates, cleaning, maintenance, repair, replacement and demolition. Only options which meet the performance requirements for the built asset should be considered.

The design team may have already considered the impact of whole-life costs on certain elements of the design. This is where the cost of maintenance is considered alongside the capital cost of the building. The Maintenance and Operational Strategy will be formulated during Stages 2 and 3, and this should enable the team to consider the costs of these activities. In some instances the client may wish to increase the budget in order to improve the specification of aspects that will reduce running costs.

WHOLE-LIFE COSTS ON A SMALL HOUSE EXTENSION

In our small house extension, the owners could install an enhanced boiler for an extra £1,000. The advance boiler produces a reduced running cost of £100 a year, therefore the payback period is ten years. The family believe that they will move in around five years' time, so on these grounds the expense may not be justified. However, the boiler improvement impacts on the overall environmental performance of the house and this could improve the selling price, allowing them to recoup the extra cost later. Providing the client with quality information is key to this design decision, and based on the information provided the family elect to put in the enhanced boiler.

Any whole-life costs studied during Stage 3 should be included in the cost plan at the stage's Information Exchange. This will ensure that the project team, at Stage 4, do not waste time revisiting decisions already determined, and that any value-engineering studies taking place during Stage 4 are well informed.

VALUE ENGINEERING

A systematic and organised approach to provide the necessary functions in a project at the lowest cost. Value engineering promotes the substitution of materials and methods with less expensive alternatives, without sacrificing functionality.

What should the status of planning be at the end of Stage 3?

At the end of Stage 3 the design will be sufficiently detailed to prepare a full planning application. Generally, before Stage 4 is commenced this application will be determined and planning permission will be achieved. The approved planning information, together with the Design and Access Statement and any other supporting documentation such as an Environmental Impact Assessment, should be included in the stage Information Exchange. In addition, it is usual when planning is granted that a number of conditions are imposed on the project. These conditions will be discharged by the project team during Stages 4 and 5.

What if planning was submitted at the end of Stage 2 Concept Design?

The RIBA Plan of Work 2013 allows the team to select when they wish to submit for planning approval. It is conceivable that a number of clients will prefer the end of Stage 2 as the submission point. This would allow them to reduce the cost of the design team, but could be a false economy. At the end of Stage 3, much more is known about the content of the design. Any plant equipment on the roof will be fully understood; materials and products can be sourced against the Project Budget. By waiting until Stage 3 the planning drawings can be more accurate in terms of scope, materials, textures and colours. If these have not been adequately covered in the application at Stage 2 it will be necessary to revisit the planners with amendments, and a significant deviation could result in a new application being requested.

WHAT SHOULD BE INCLUDED IN THE
Information Exchange at the end of Stage 3?

Once all the tasks in a stage are completed, the project team prepare the information for handing on to the next stage. This is an important gateway as all the information should be complete before the next stage can commence. It is good practice to ensure the client signs off the design at these gateways, so that the RIBA Plan of Work 2013 stages are respected and abortive work is avoided. Within the Information Exchange at the end of Stage 3 Developed Design, it should be possible to review the following:

- Design information (drawings and/or models). These should be at an appropriate scale, say 1:100 to 1:50 if produced in CAD. The level of detail in a BIM environment should be sufficient to allow all services and structure to be coordinated between architecture, structure and building-service disciplines. The coordinated design must align with the cost information.
- The Project Budget. This should be broken down by element, so that it is apparent what has been included in the cost. Accuracy should be to +/- 10%.
- The procurement route. This should have been determined. If a single-stage design and build contract has been selected, then the Employer's Requirements will form part of the Information Exchange at the end of the stage.
- All health and safety implications will have been considered by the design team, and risk registers completed.
- A number of key Project Strategy documents will be included for updating. These will cover sustainability, maintenance and operation, handover, construction and health and safety.
- The Project Execution Plan. This will have been updated, and relevant control procedures will be in place.
- Planning. A submission would typically take place using the documentation produced for this stage's Information Exchange. Obtaining planning permission may be a prerequisite to starting Stage 4.

- A Project Programme. This should show the duration allowed for the subsequent stages of the project.
- A Design Programme. This should show the duration required to produce the appropriate level of detail during the Technical Design.

On many projects there is a requirement to complete the building as quickly as possible. Moving at speed increases the risk that the design will not be fully resolved before construction has commenced. Even though it may be possible to overlap the start of Stage 4 with the end of Stage 3, this can only be achieved if the information is produced in packages or work sections. This will result in a sequential completion of Stage 3.

OVERLAPPING STAGES

Let us look at the development of Scenario E, our high-tech office building. As the building is required to be completed in a short period of time, the client has adopted a management contract for the project. Before the design team have finalised the interior design for the building, the contractor wants to start the foundations and superstructure. By dealing with each element as a package it is possible to achieve this. As the design reaches the end of Stage 3 and is coordinated, the structural engineer can commence Stage 4 on these early packages. Of course, the risk to the design team is that as the Developed Design is completed more becomes known about the building, which may affect the structure and result in abortive work. The potential for these risks to occur should be highlighted to the client before this kind of acceleration is commenced. To mitigate these risks the lead designer can adopt a robust design strategy, which either incorporates flexibility in design – such as by allowing adequate zones for services development – or versatility in design by understanding the constraints that need to be adopted.

The diagram in Figure 1.2 illustrates the following:

- Design work on foundations, superstructure and cladding is complete.
- Construction work is due to commence on the structure.
- The cladding package is out to tender.
- The design team are still working on all the interior packages.
- Multiple Information Exchanges as each package comes to conclusion.

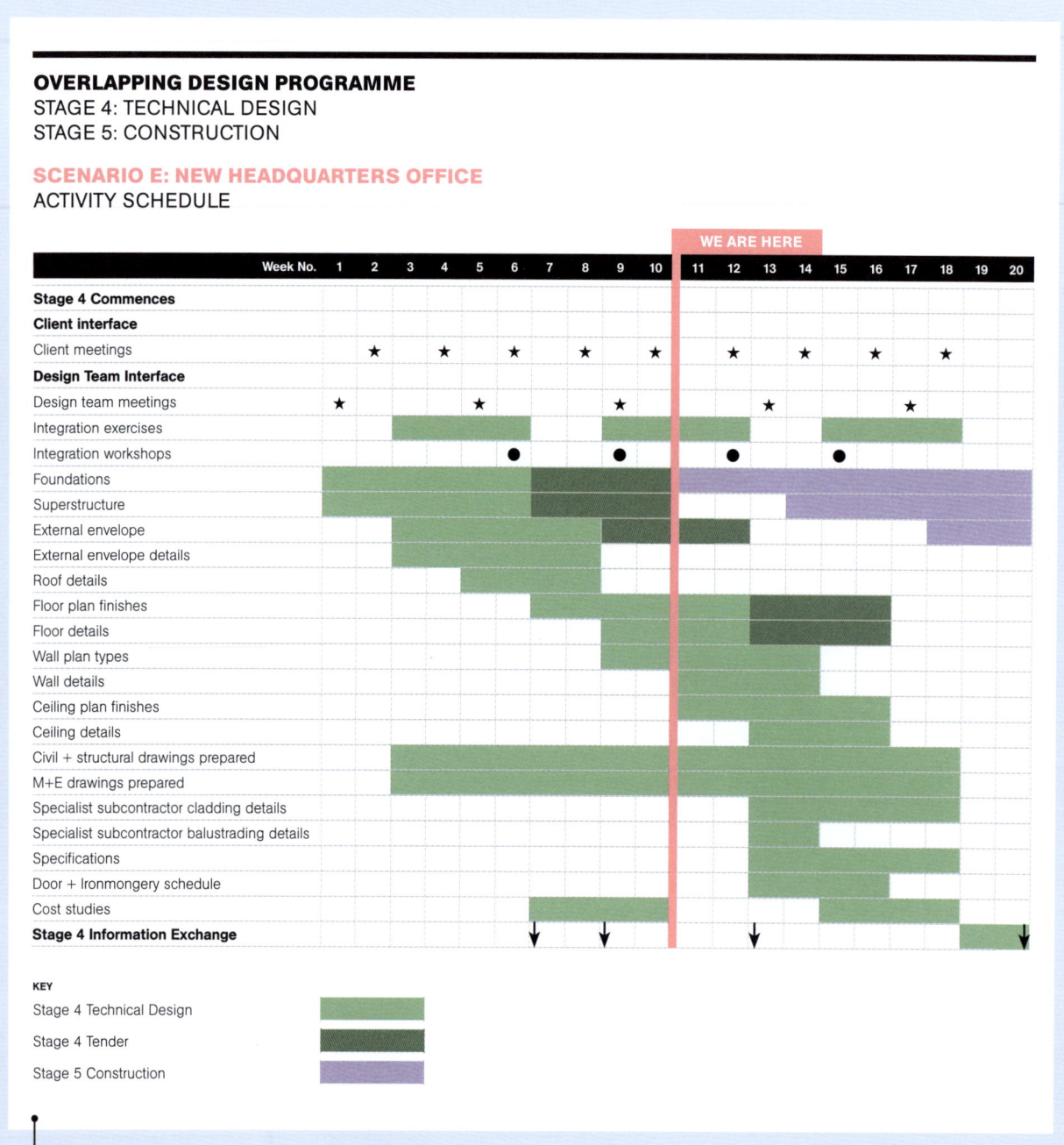

1.2

An overlapping design and construction programme.

SUMMARY

We are now in a good position to commence Stage 4. We have explained what to expect at the end of Stage 3: what the status of the Developed Design information should be, and what to expect in the Information Exchange. Once we commence Technical Design we do not expect to revisit design decisions taken throughout Stages 2 and 3, so it is important that the client signs off the end of Stage 3. When dealing with a complex client consisting of multiple stakeholders, this is best done through an end of stage presentation. In all instances a good Developed Design report will capture all the decisions made by the design team in producing the building design. In the next chapter we will examine what happens at the start of Stage 4.

SCENARIO SUMMARIES

WHAT HAS HAPPENED TO OUR PROJECTS BY THE END OF STAGE 3?

Small residential extension for a growing family

The design team have completed coordinated design. A full planning application is prepared and submitted to the local authority. In line with the traditional procurement route the architect has started to sound out the interest of local builders to tender. A number have full order books and the architect has been contacting colleagues to find some other suitable builders as well as taking references to provide to the client.

Development of five new homes for a small residential developer

The developer obtained planning permission at Stage 2, so where the design has changed slightly during Stage 3 the architect has had to resubmit it to the local planning officer for approval. Fortunately the changes were minor in nature, and the planning officer was able to approve the changes himself through delegated powers. The developer has continued to drive down the budget for the scheme through amendments to the outline specification, but has eventually signed off the design and the cost plan. The developer has confirmed that a traditional contract is the preferred procurement route.

Refurbishment of a teaching and support building for a university

The university have elected to procure the building through a single-stage design and build contract. The contractor has been selected and the design team have been novated. Initial surveys to open up the existing fabric have been undertaken and the design team have used this information in the development of a coordinated design. There are still some areas of concern that the design team were unable to examine prior to construction, and these have been included in the risk register. An enhanced contingency figure has been retained by the university to cover the cost of any unforeseen works that may come to light in Stage 4.

New central library for a small unitary authority

The client's design team have worked closely with the contractor's design team throughout Stage 3 to ensure that the Project Objectives are being met. The contractor has finally been appointed under a two-stage design and build contract after finalising the method of construction and firming up his lump-sum price. Working through Stage 3 has enabled the contractor to influence the method of construction, and the external envelope is to be prefabricated off site. This has enabled the contractor to offer a reduction in the Stage 5 Construction Programme.

A fully developed design report, together with a fixed lump-sum price for the works, has been prepared and signed off by the authority. The specification is an outline one at this stage, although the client's design team have obtained confirmation from the contractor on 80% of the proposed materials and finishes. Which are included in the Contractor's Proposals included in the Building Contract.

New headquarters office for high-tech internet-based company

The client signed off the design at the end of Stage 3 and submitted for planning permission. Because they are keen to progress the project quickly, they instructed the commencement of Stage 4 before planning was obtained. The work is divided into 15 different packages so that work can commence sooner on the earlier packages.

The construction manager produces a cost estimate for the project that is within 10% of the budget. He market-tests some of the major packages such as cladding prior to Stage 4 commencing. The Handover Strategy is developed in detail with the client, as they wish to fit some of their own equipment in the building towards the end of the project.

CHAPTER 02

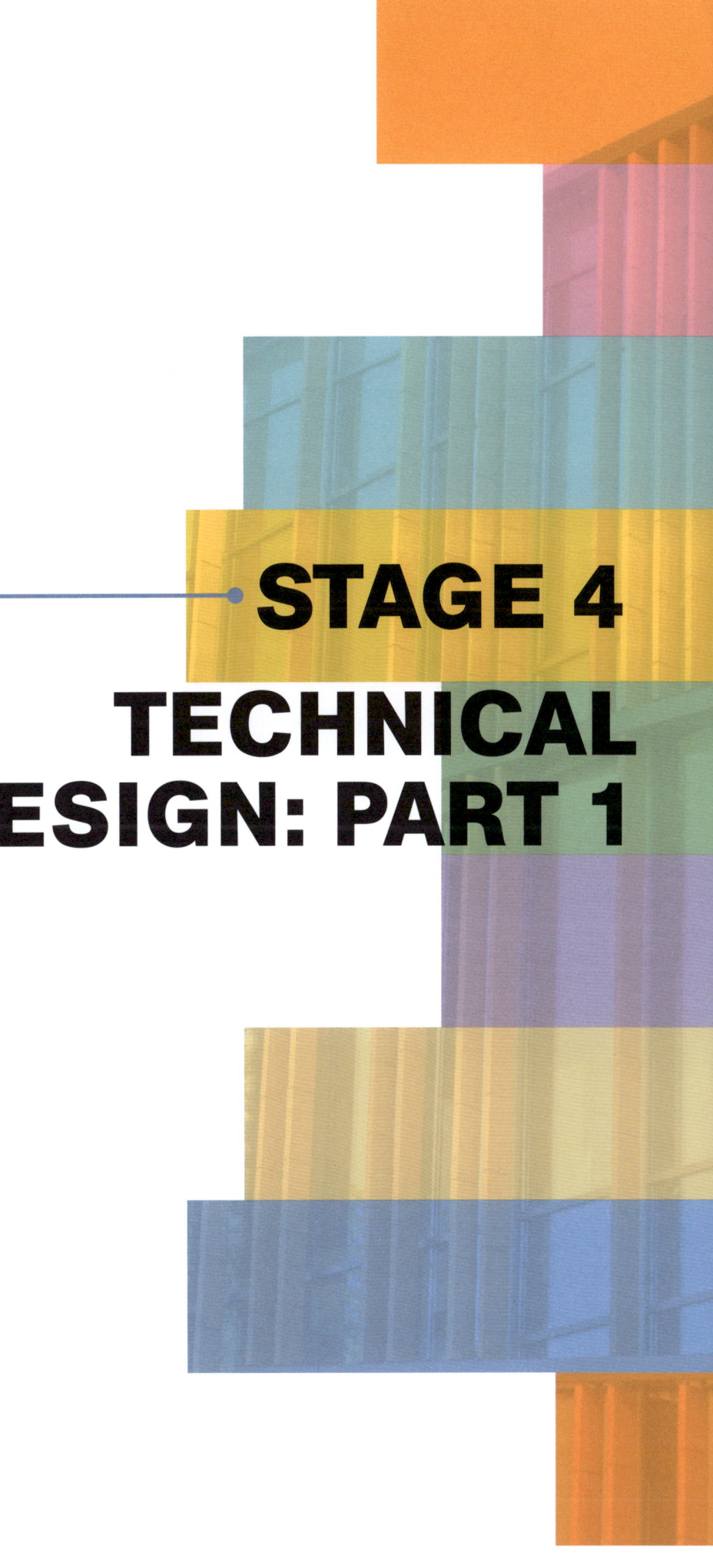

STAGE 4
TECHNICAL DESIGN: PART 1

RIBA
Plan of
Work
2013

Stage 4

Technical
Design

Task Bar	Tasks
Core Objectives	Prepare **Technical Design** in accordance with **Design Responsibility Matrix** and **Project Strategies** to include all architectural, structural and building services information, specialist subcontractor design and specifications, in accordance with **Design Programme**.
Procurement *Variable task bar*	*The Procurement activities during this stage will depend on the procurement route determined during Stage 1.*
Programme *Variable task bar*	*The RIBA Plan of Work 2013 enables this stage to overlap with a number of other stages depending on the selected procurement route.*
(Town) Planning *Variable task bar*	*The RIBA Plan of Work 2013 suggests that any conditions attached to a planning consent are addressed during this stage, prior to work starting on site during Stage 5.*
Suggested Key Support Tasks	Review and update **Sustainability, Maintenance and Operational** and **Handover Strategies** and **Risk Assessments**. Prepare and submit Building Regulations submission and any other third party submissions requiring consent. Review and update **Project Execution Plan**. Review **Construction Strategy**, including sequencing, and update **Health and Safety Strategy**. *A further review of the **Project Strategies** and documentation previously generated is required during this stage.*
Sustainability Checkpoints	• *Is the formal sustainability assessment substantially complete?* • *Have details been audited for airtightness and continuity of insulation?* • *Has the Building Regulations Part L submission been made and the design stage carbon/energy declaration been updated and the future climate impact assessment prepared?* • *Has a non-technical user guide been drafted and have the format and content of the Part L log book been agreed?* • *Has all outstanding design stage sustainability assessment information been submitted?* • *Are building **Handover Strategy** and monitoring technologies specified?* • *Have the implications of changes to the specification or design been reviewed against agreed sustainability criteria?* • *Has compliance of agreed sustainability criteria for contributions by specialist subcontractors been demonstrated?*
Information Exchanges (at stage completion)	Completed **Technical Design** of the project.
UK Government Information Exchanges	Not required.

OVERVIEW

Having produced a coordinated design at Stage 3, it is now time to develop the Technical Design of the building. Initially the Technical Design information will represent the design intent of the design team, and as specialist subcontractors become part of the team the details will incorporate the components and products that the building is to be constructed from. Exactly how far to take the Technical Design will depend on whether the construction on site will be based on the information produced by the design team or on the information to be developed by a specialist subcontractor. In any event it is more than likely that the architect will be active as the lead designer and asked to coordinate all of the design work, and in many instances this will mean ensuring that the information describing the building is fully representative of the final detail. To do this accurately they will need to know who is doing each activity, and when they are delivering their Technical Designs.

This chapter will explain how to get started on the Stage 4 Technical Design. It will describe what level of information needs to be provided at this stage; how to adjust the Design Responsibility Matrix, if necessary; and how to develop a Design Programme for this stage. Many of the decisions taken during Stage 4 are affected by the procurement route selected at Stage 2 or 3, and within this chapter there is an explanation of how this selection affects Stage 4.

In the next chapter we will examine in more detail the key support tasks that the project team will need to complete, and clarify what should be in the Sustainability Checkpoints and Information Exchanges at the end of Stage 4. There is also a description of the key items that the project team will need to consider during Technical Design. Whilst in practice Stages 4 and 5 will overlap for most projects, the work on an individual package or section of the design must be complete at Stage 4 before Stage 5 Construction can commence.

WHAT IS STAGE 4?

The core objectives for Stage 4 are:

- To complete the Technical Design required for all architectural, civil, structural, building services and specialist subcontractor information to be ready for construction, allowing for any overlap between Stages 4 and 5.
- To clarify who is responsible for each and every item of the Technical Design.
- To develop a new Design Programme in order to ensure that the stage is completed in a timely manner.

Having defined the Project Objectives during Stage 1, it is important that the technical solutions are defined in sufficient detail to ensure that those objectives can be delivered. Just as in earlier stages, it is important that the project lead continually tests the project's development against the Quality Objectives and Project Outcomes previously developed.

Throughout Technical Design the project is developed to ensure that architectural, building services and structural engineering designs are refined to a level that will enable construction to take place. At the conclusion of Stage 4, the following will have been achieved:

- The project team will have completed a fully integrated set of technical information sufficient for construction.
- The cost consultant will have completed an updated construction cost estimate that is fully integrated with the Technical Design information.
- The specialist subcontractors will have completed their design, and it will be integrated into the construction documentation.
- All disciplines will have completed their technical details.
- The Construction Strategy will have been finalised and will be understood by all.
- Any planning conditions will have been discharged.
- All statutory approvals required from the design team will have been secured.

IS A CONSTRUCTION COST ESTIMATE USEFUL AT STAGE 4?

The benefit of keeping the construction cost estimate up to date is that it ensures that the client is fully aware of the cost of the building before he of she goes to tender. However, it may prove more expedient under a traditional contract to replace the pre-tender estimate at Stage 4 with a real construction price for the works. Should this price prove to be in excess of previous estimates, then value-engineering studies can be undertaken with the preferred contractor to produce the optimum result.

The detail in Figure 2.1 (overleaf) illustrates:

- The relationship between the primary structure, the structural floor, the finishes and the balustrading system.
- That the specialist subcontractor would be expected to produce fabrication drawings for the balustrading based on the architect's technical design intentions.
- That the architect would be expected to provide integrated construction details for the flooring, acoustically insulated fascia and service tray, the last-named of which may be a proprietary product.

Preparing for Stage 4

Before embarking on Stage 4 it is important to ensure that the following actions have been completed:

- The Stage 3 design has been signed off by the client.
- The architectural, structural and building services designs have been coordinated.
- The fee for Stage 4 has been agreed with the client (where this has not already been agreed, as recommended, at Stage 1).
- The Information Exchanges for the stage have been clearly defined.
- A Design Programme for the completion of the integrated Technical Design has been agreed, including the work of the specialist subcontractors.
- The Design Responsibility Matrix has been adjusted to align with the contractor's final position on the role of any specialist subcontractors.
- The appropriate resources have been identified.

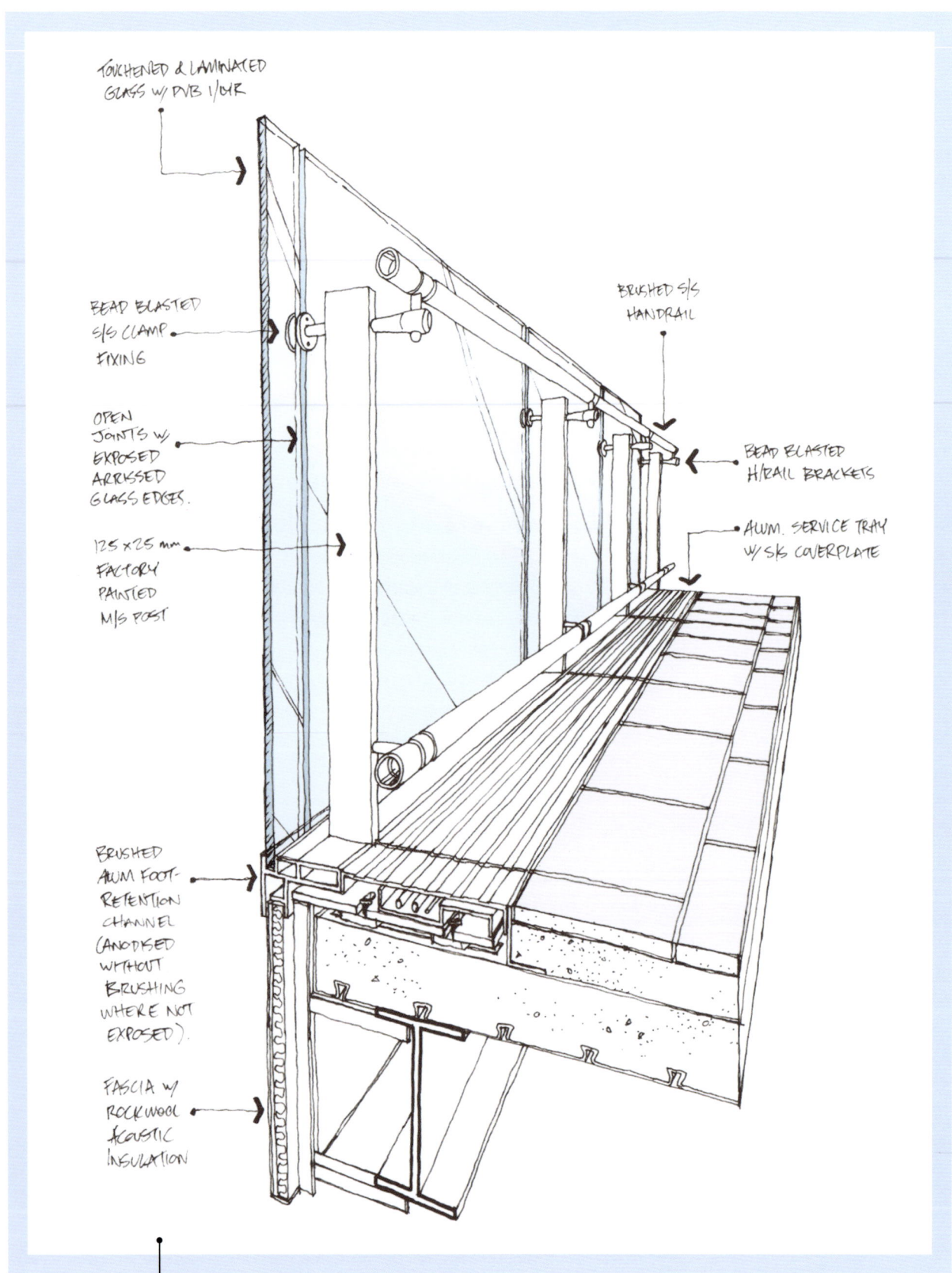

TOUGHENED & LAMINATED
GLASS W/ PVB I/DUR

BRUSHED S/S
HANDRAIL

BEAD BLASTED
S/S CLAMP
FIXING

OPEN
JOINTS W/
EXPOSED
ARRISSED
GLASS EDGES.

BEAD BLASTED
H/RAIL BRACKETS

125 x 25 mm
FACTORY
PAINTED
M/S POST

ALUM. SERVICE TRAY
W/ S/S COVERPLATE

BRUSHED
ALUM FOOT-
RETENTION
CHANNEL
(ANODISED
WITHOUT
BRUSHING
WHERE NOT
EXPOSED).

FASCIA W/
ROCKWOOL
ACOUSTIC
INSULATION

2.1
An example of the level of detail
produced for Stage 4.

How do you select the level of detail to be included in the information to be exchanged at the end of Stage 4?

The level of detail to be included in the Information Exchange needs to be carefully considered. The information needs to be sufficient to describe the full scope of the works that the contractor is going to carry out. Although CAD information is produced 'full size', it is typically issued or exchanged in 'hard' (prints) or 'soft' (electronic) formats with the level of detail added to the CAD model dictated by the scale of the output (eg 1:100, 1:50, 1:5). BIM will change this approach, and whilst it is likely that 2D 'slices' through the model will continue to be used for construction purposes for some time the requirement to provide fully digital information as a means of communicating with the fabricator is already a reality. As with CAD information, it is preferable to restrict the level of detail in the model to match the purpose of the output.

LEVEL OF DETAIL

On drawings that need to illustrate the fire compartmentation of a building, it will not be necessary to show the cladding extrusions of the curtain walling. The level of detail required would be commensurate with a plan produced at 1:100.

General-arrangement information will have been inherited from Stage 3. This will range in scale from 1:200 to 1:50 depending on the size of the project. It should now be enhanced to include setting-out dimensions, enabling the contractor to position all components in the building accurately. References should also be included to key components for scheduling purposes, and to larger-scale drawings. Where specialist subcontractors are going to be engaged to complete the drawings, then details only need to be prepared to show the design intent. Where there is no requirement for specialist subcontractors, the design team will need to draw the construction details at a typical scale, ranging from 1:20 to 1:5; in practice, this will be the point at which full-size details in CAD or BIM are appropriate to generate the output.

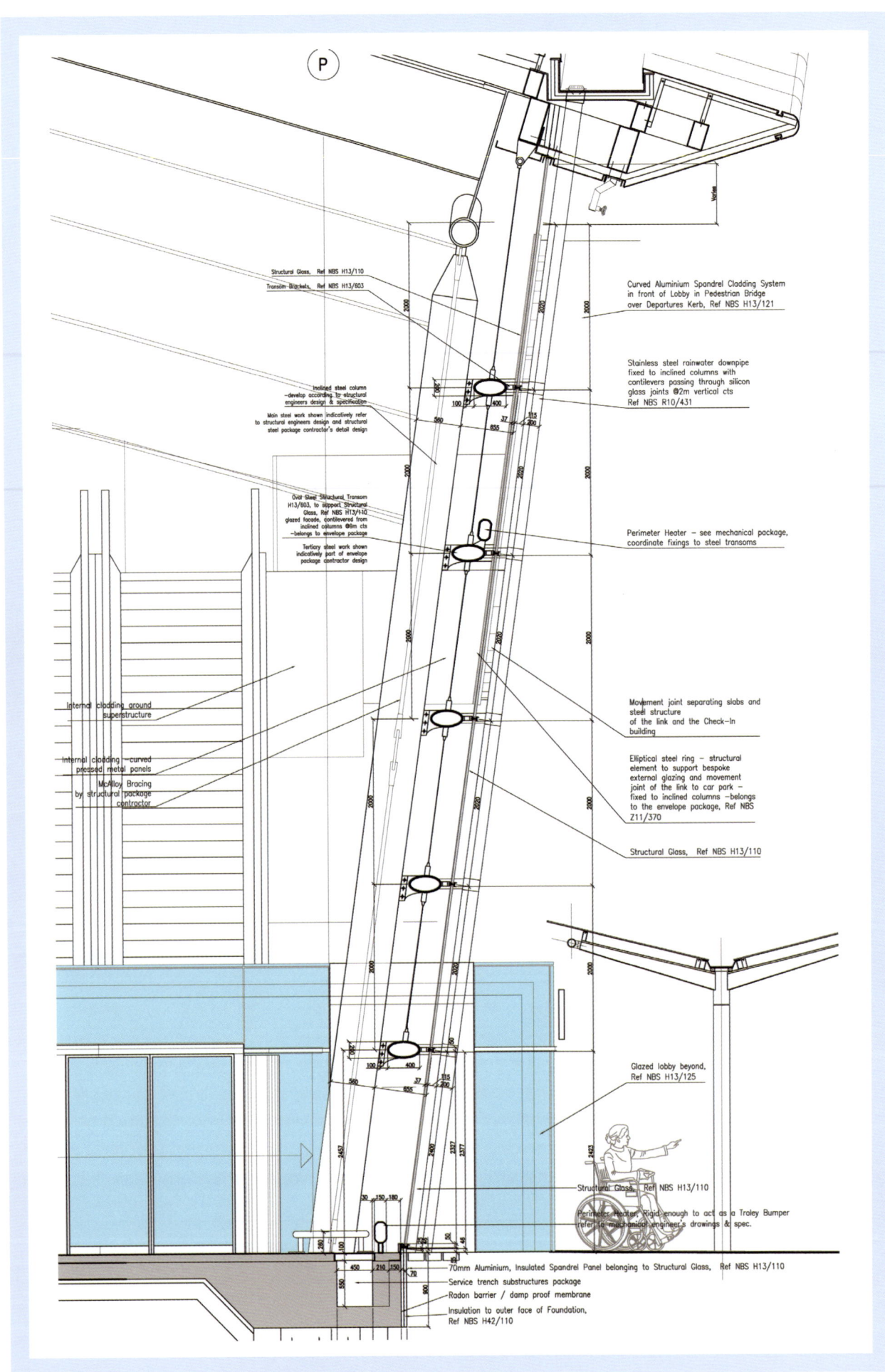

P

Structural Glass, Ref NBS H13/110
Transom Brackets, Ref NBS H13/803

Inclined steel column
—develop according to structural
engineers design & specification

Main steel work shown indicatively refer
to structural engineers design and structural
steel package contractor's detail design

Oval Steel Structural Transom
H13/803, to support Structural
Glass, Ref NBS H13/110
glazed facade, cantilevered from
inclined columns @6m cts
—belongs to envelope package

Tertiary steel work shown
indicatively part of envelope
package contractor design

Internal cladding around
superstructure

Internal cladding —curved
pressed metal panels

McAlloy Bracing
by structural package
contractor

Curved Aluminium Spandrel Cladding System
in front of Lobby in Pedestrian Bridge
over Departures Kerb, Ref NBS H13/121

Stainless steel rainwater downpipe
fixed to inclined columns with
contilevers passing through silicon
glass joints @2m vertical cts
Ref NBS R10/431

Perimeter Heater – see mechanical package,
coordinate fixings to steel transoms

Movement joint separating slabs and
steel structure
of the link and the Check–In
building

Elliptical steel ring – structural
element to support bespoke
external glazing and movement
joint of the link to car park –
fixed to inclined columns —belongs
to the envelope package, Ref NBS
Z11/370

Structural Glass, Ref NBS H13/110

Glazed lobby beyond,
Ref NBS H13/125

Structural Glass, Ref NBS H13/110

Perimeter Heater, Rigid enough to act as a Trolley Bumper
refer to mechanical engineer's drawings & spec.

70mm Aluminium, Insulated Spandrel Panel belonging to Structural Glass, Ref NBS H13/110
Service trench substructures package
Radon barrier / damp proof membrane
Insulation to outer face of Foundation,
Ref NBS H42/110

2.2
Sketch (right) illustrating design model received in the Information Exchange at the end of Stage 3, together with the Technical Design drawing (facing page) prepared by the design team at Stage 4.

The design information in Figure 2.2 (previous page) illustrates the development of a complex project facade by Pascall+Watson architects. The information shows that:

- By the end of Stage 3 the relationship between facade, structure and roof edge has been coordinated.
- The sizes of glass panels and the transom positions have been fixed.
- At Stage 4 this information is conveyed at a larger scale than hitherto. Setting-out geometry is also shown on the drawing.
- All the major components are described, and extrusion shapes and sizes for the steelwork components are illustrated.
- The drawing is capable of enlargement to 1:5, although not everything is illustrated in full.

HOW TO DETERMINE IF THE INFORMATION SHOULD BE EXCHANGED IN A DIGITAL FORMAT

The development of BIM has enabled the design team to deliver their information to the contractor in digital format. In some instances, this digital information will be used directly by the fabricator. An example might be laser-cut steelwork connections or digital information that can be used to generate complex mouldings. It is important that the design team understand the fabrication strategy so that they are able to deliver the information in the correct format.

In order to complete the Technical Design, a detailed integration exercise will need to be undertaken. Whether this is done through the recommended route of using a three-dimensional model or utilising drawing overlays, it is essential that all the designers complete information to a similar level of scale and detail. This should be agreed during the confirmation of appointments at the start of Stage 4.

SCENARIO C: THE REFURBISHMENT OF A TEACHING AND SUPPORT BUILDING FOR A UNIVERSITY

At Stage 4, the architect will produce drawings illustrating the ceiling layouts. These will show the existing structure and the size of void available above the ceiling. In order to complete the detailed coordination of the building information the lead designer will need accurate drawings of the mechanical and electrical (M+E) installations, showing ducts and cable runs. It is at Stage 4, when the specialist subcontractors join the design team, that this type of information becomes available. These should be drawn to include the thickness of any insulation around the duct. See Figure 2.3 (overleaf) for an example of a detailed coordination model.

The drawing in Figure 2.3 (overleaf) illustrates the position of ductwork and the provision of underfloor trunking. The structure is a flat slab with a structural upstand, and the zone for services is agreed. The next level of coordination will be required to position the raised-floor support points and any ductwork hangers. This kind of information can be covered by standard details from the specialist subcontractor.

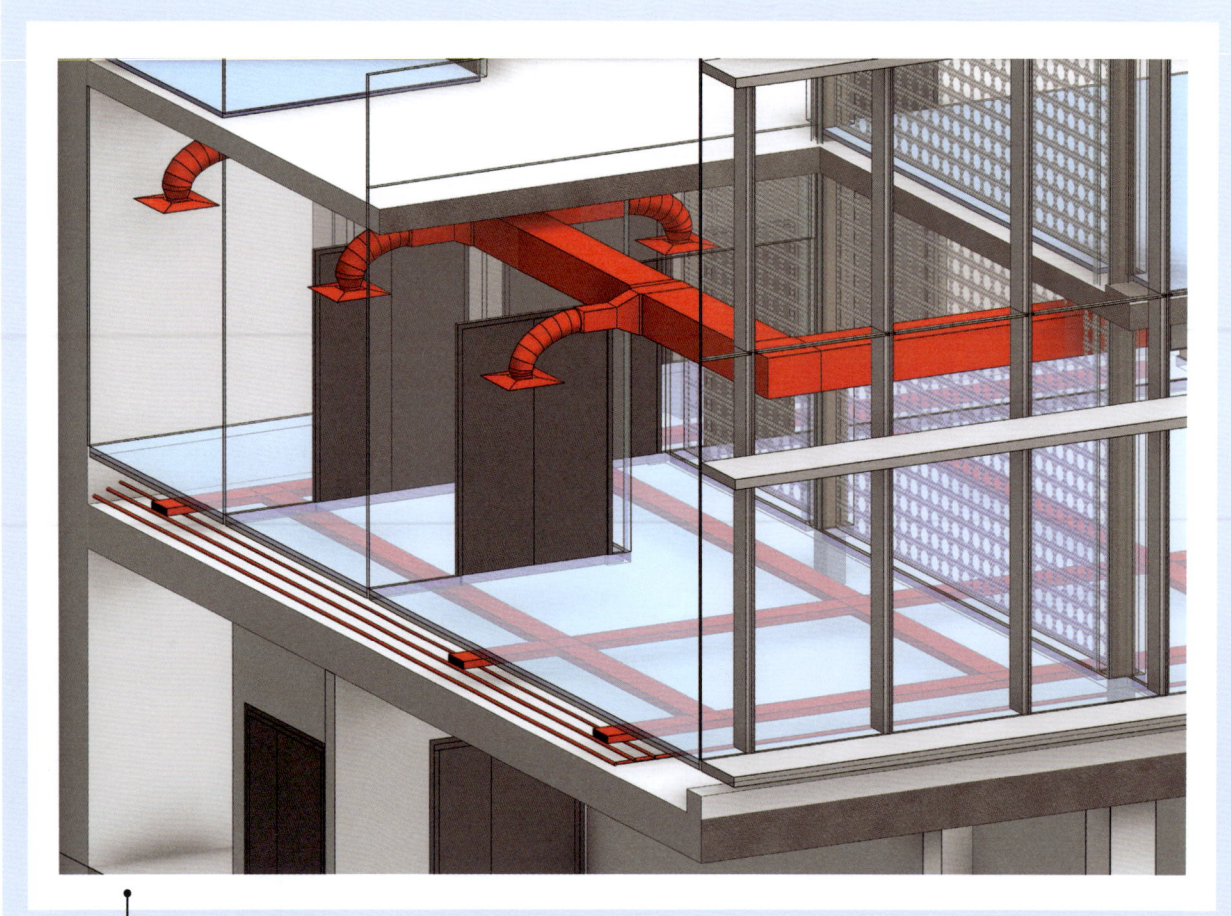

2.3
A Stage 4 model
illustrating the
relationship of
the services with
the structure and
envelope.

What is the difference between design work produced by the design team and that produced by specialist subcontractors?

The overall aim of both the design team and the specialist subcontractor is the same: to provide information to the contractor to enable them to complete construction. There are, however, some differences between their approaches. The design team produce design-intent details when working with specialist subcontractors. These show relationships between components, key setting-out dimensions and interfaces with other products. The specialist subcontractor can insert their real component into these design-intent details. They will also produce fabrication drawings for the manufacture of each component. These drawings are used by off-site manufacturers to build their product. There may be a requirement for the design team to sign these off before manufacture can commence.

DEVELOPING A PERFORMANCE SPECIFICATION

Many modern cladding systems are developed to a high degree of sophistication in order to combat temperature fluctuations, thermal bridges, acoustic performance, water penetration and air filtration standards. It is unlikely that an architect will design their own bespoke cladding system for a project. What they can develop, however, is a performance specification describing the standard to be achieved from the cladding. This can be supplemented with drawings illustrating the appearance of the cladding, the size of panels, the depth of members, etc. It can also be enhanced by design-intent details that illustrate the relationship of the cladding to the structure, ceiling, walls and floors. Prospective cladding companies can then use their specialist skills and knowledge to develop these design-intent details into construction information.

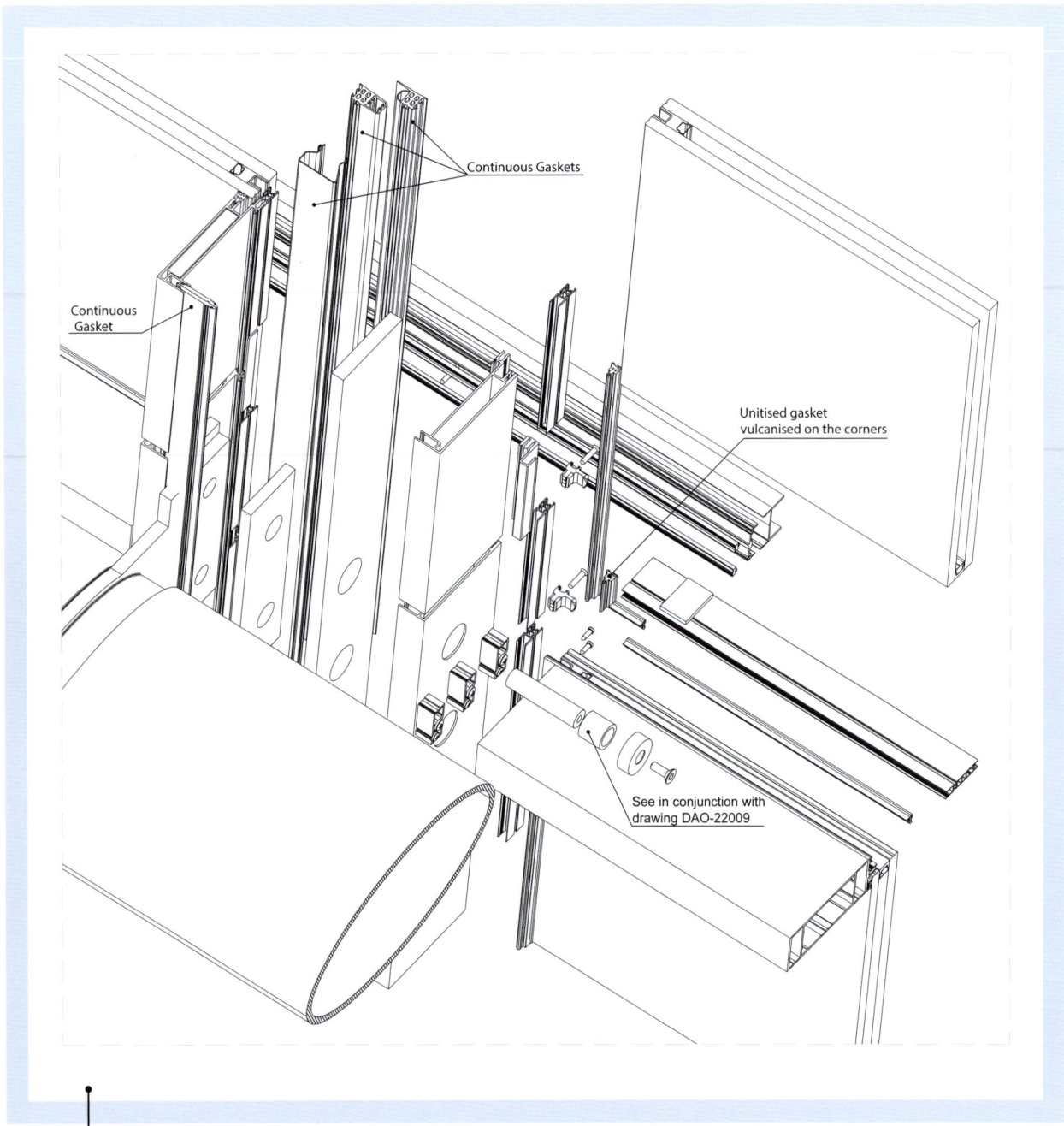

Continuous Gaskets

Continuous
Gasket

Unitised gasket
vulcanised on the corners

See in conjunction with
drawing DAO-22009

2.4

A specialist subcontractor
drawing for the elevation
in Figure 2.2.

The specifications produced by the design team and the specialist subcontractor are also different. The design team will set out the performance standard that the specialist is expected to meet. The specialist will specify the standard that the selected product is able to achieve.

SCENARIO E: NEW OFFICE FOR HIGH-TECH INTERNET-BASED COMPANY

By way of example: the design team of our high-tech office specify a single membrane for the flat roof. It needs to be waterproof and resistant to temperature fluctuations; it must be capable of draining to rainwater outlets without ponding. All of these items and others can be described in a performance specification. The roof specialist will select a product that will satisfy the performance standard. His specification will describe the constraining characteristics of the chosen material, how the product is to be laid, the characteristics of the material and the tolerances required for movement, the type of support layer and how falls are to be achieved. It is important that when the design team review this specification, they confirm that all the performance requirements are met.

How do we make sure that the information is produced at the right time?

To ensure that the information is produced at the right time by all members of the design team, it is essential to update the Design Programme and implement the Design Responsibility Matrix. Having both of these in place will enable the project lead to ensure the successful completion of Stage 4. It will also assist monitoring of progress throughout the stage.

APPOINTING CONSULTANTS

Ensure that all the design team members are appointed and the full scope of works for Technical Design is allocated before commencing this stage. Delivering a fully integrated design is a complex task, and it will rely on all disciplines working to an agreed Design Programme. This will ensure that the appropriate information is available at the right time.

What is the relationship between the Project Programme, the Design Programme and the Construction Programme?

The overall Project Programme prepared at Stage 0 will determine the amount of time available for each stage. It will acknowledge the procurement route for the project, and may even illustrate an overlap between Stage 4 and Stage 5. The Design Programme determines the amount of time available to complete the design activities contained within each stage. It will illustrate the work of the design team to ensure that the design is completed in a logical manner. The Construction Programme is developed as Stage 4 progresses, and should be complete by the start of Stage 5. It will show the period of time required to procure, deliver and construct each component of the project after the design is complete.

Developing a Design Programme

There are numerous software packages that assist in graphically presenting a Design Programme for this stage, and they are generally predicated on a sequential production of the project deliverables. As the design is already coordinated with the core design team members, the development of the Technical Design information often follows the construction logic. In this way the plans are developed first, from the foundations up to roof level. Simultaneously with the plans, larger sections and elevations are developed. As the technical documentation progresses the design team will need to develop more detailed information in order that the contractor can fully appreciate how different components are expected to come together. Eventually the design work of the specialist subcontractors will be integrated into the Technical Design, and the time that they require to produce their documentation will need to be identified in the Technical Design programme.

DESIGN PROGRAMME
STAGE 4 PROGRAMME

SCENARIO D: NEW CENTRAL LIBRARY
ACTIVITY SCHEDULE

Week No.	1	2	3	4	5	6	7	8	9	10	11	12	13	14	15	16	17	18	19	20
Stage 4 commences	↓																			
Client interface																				
Client meetings		★		★		★		★		★		★		★		★		★		
Design team interface																				
Design team meetings	★				★				★				★				★			
Integration exercises			▓	▓	▓	▓			▓	▓	▓			▓	▓	▓	▓	▓		
Integration workshops						●			●			●			●					
Architectural plans developed	▓	▓	▓																	
Architectural sections developed	▓	▓	▓	▓																
Architectural elevations developed			▓	▓	▓	▓														
External envelope details				▓	▓	▓														
Roof details					▓	▓														
Floor plan finishes						▓	▓	▓												
Floor details							▓	▓	▓											
Wall plan types								▓	▓	▓										
Wall details									▓	▓	▓									
Ceiling plan finishes											▓	▓	▓							
Ceiling details												▓	▓	▓						
Civil + structural drawings prepared			▓	▓	▓	▓	▓	▓	▓	▓	▓	▓	▓	▓	▓	▓	▓	▓		
M+E drawings prepared			▓	▓	▓	▓	▓	▓	▓	▓	▓	▓	▓	▓	▓	▓	▓	▓		
Specialist subcontractor cladding details											▓	▓	▓	▓	▓					
Specialist subcontractor balustrading details													▓	▓	▓	▓				
Specifications														▓	▓	▓	▓			
Door + ironmongery schedule									▓	▓	▓									
Cost studies						▓	▓	▓	▓				▓	▓	▓					
Stage 4 Information Exchange																				▓ ↓

2.5
An example of a Stage 4 Technical Design programme.

This example of a Stage 4 programme:

- Clearly shows the start of the stage and the end point, when the project team information will be issued for construction.
- Illustrates the variety of meetings and workshops that may be expected at this stage.
- Represents the logical sequence for the production of information that can be applied to a building project.
- Sets out when the specialist subcontractors will complete their drawings.
- Contains a two-week contingency period (weeks 19 and 20) to ensure that all information is complete and checked prior to its final issue.

WHAT IMPACT CAN DIFFERENT PROCUREMENT ROUTES HAVE ON THE DESIGN PROGRAMME AT STAGE 4?

The desire to complete projects quickly can lead to a situation where early packages of work are fixed and tendered before later packages have been concluded. This can happen in either a management contract or a design and build contract. It often means that the design team are constrained in their options as the Technical Design develops; this is referred to as progressive fixity. There is also an impact on the programme if two-stage or single-stage design and build is used. As part of the contractor's proposals in design and build contracts, the contractor may be asked to include the Technical Design of key packages such as steelwork or cladding. If this is the case the Design Programme will usually show an overlap between Stages 4 and 5, and it will also identify the critical path through the programme. In a traditional contract the information is developed in the same logical pattern, but it is all completed before the project is tendered.

CRITICAL PATH

A critical path defines those activities in a project plan which must be completed before the next activity on the critical path can start. If there is a delay for a day on a critical path activity then the entire project could be delayed for a day.

It is useful to represent the production of information in a summarised way on the Design Programme. For instance, it generally makes sense for all the documentation for the external envelope to be grouped together. In a similar way, all the details for the internal joinery or ceilings can be grouped. A useful checklist at this stage may include the following packages:

- Demolition/alteration/renovation.
- Groundwork.
- In situ concrete.
- Masonry.
- Structural metal/timber.
- Cladding/covering.
- Waterproofing.
- Linings/sheathing/dry partitioning.
- Windows/doors/stairs.
- Surface finishes.
- Furniture/equipment.
- External works.
- Drainage systems.
- Mechanical systems.
- Electrical systems.

On complex projects a simple Design Programme may be insufficient to ensure that the work is undertaken in the correct sequence. To improve the project team's understanding of their contribution to Technical Design, a technique called process mapping can be used. Process mapping comprises a workflow diagram that is used to clarify the work activities involved in a process or series of processes. It represents the design as a linear process, in which key inputs to each activity have to be completed before that activity can be started (see Figure 2.6 overleaf).

A PROCESS MAP FOR DETAILING

The activity of detailing the balustrading shown at the start of this chapter cannot be commenced until the structure below the slab is known, the budget for the system is agreed, and the method of procurement and the anticipated construction methodology is understood. A detailed process map can capture the inputs required to achieve those tasks and catalogue the outputs expected.

2.6

A Level 1 process map for the technical design of a complex project.

LEVEL 1 ACTIVITIES/DELIVERABLES PLAN
STAGE 4: TECHNICAL DESIGN

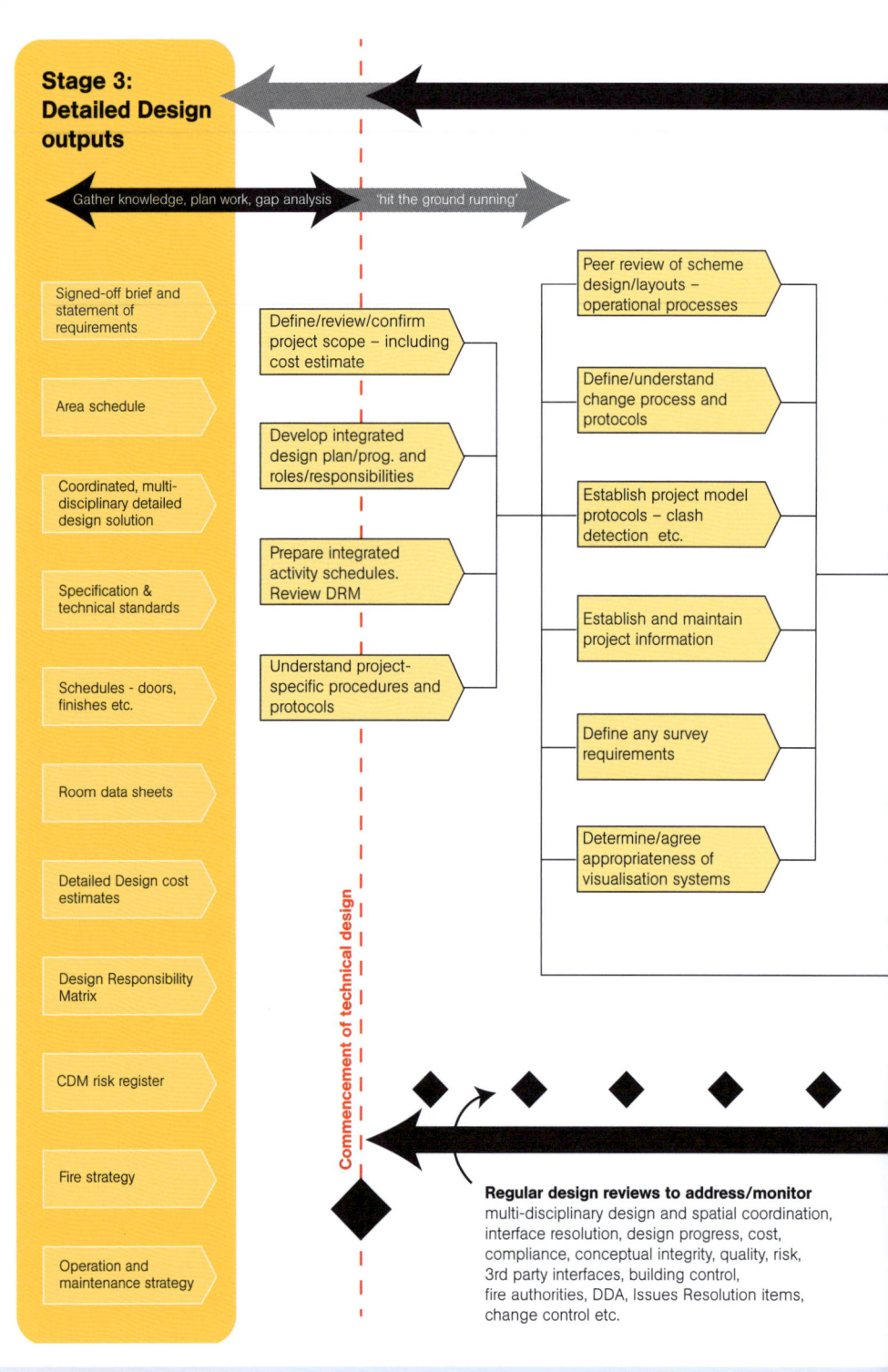

Stage 3: Detailed Design outputs

Gather knowledge, plan work, gap analysis

'hit the ground running'

Signed-off brief and statement of requirements

Area schedule

Coordinated, multi-disciplinary detailed design solution

Specification & technical standards

Schedules - doors, finishes etc.

Room data sheets

Detailed Design cost estimates

Design Responsibility Matrix

CDM risk register

Fire strategy

Operation and maintenance strategy

Define/review/confirm project scope – including cost estimate

Develop integrated design plan/prog. and roles/responsibilities

Prepare integrated activity schedules. Review DRM

Understand project-specific procedures and protocols

Peer review of scheme design/layouts – operational processes

Define/understand change process and protocols

Establish project model protocols – clash detection etc.

Establish and maintain project information

Define any survey requirements

Determine/agree appropriateness of visualisation systems

Commencement of technical design

Regular design reviews to address/monitor
multi-disciplinary design and spatial coordination, interface resolution, design progress, cost, compliance, conceptual integrity, quality, risk, 3rd party interfaces, building control, fire authorities, DDA, Issues Resolution items, change control etc.

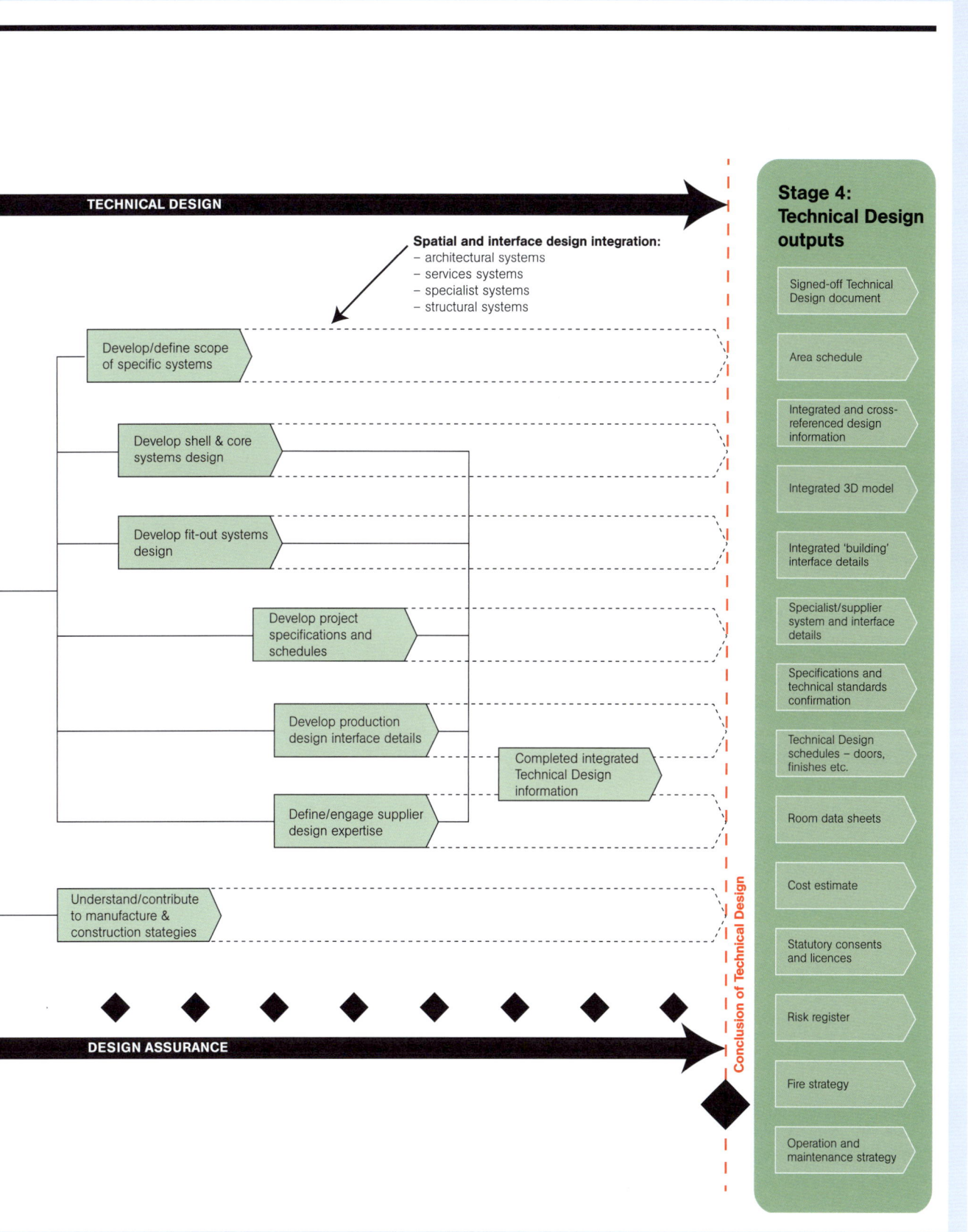

TECHNICAL DESIGN

Spatial and interface design integration:
– architectural systems
– services systems
– specialist systems
– structural systems

Develop/define scope of specific systems

Develop shell & core systems design

Develop fit-out systems design

Develop project specifications and schedules

Develop production design interface details

Completed integrated Technical Design information

Define/engage supplier design expertise

Understand/contribute to manufacture & construction stategies

DESIGN ASSURANCE

Conclusion of Technical Design

Stage 4: Technical Design outputs

Signed-off Technical Design document

Area schedule

Integrated and cross-referenced design information

Integrated 3D model

Integrated 'building' interface details

Specialist/supplier system and interface details

Specifications and technical standards confirmation

Technical Design schedules – doors, finishes etc.

Room data sheets

Cost estimate

Statutory consents and licences

Risk register

Fire strategy

Operation and maintenance strategy

How do you monitor the Design Programme?

It is important throughout Stage 4 to keep track of progress. Many of the software packages available for preparing a design programme enable you to calculate the achieved progress. On smaller projects, a simple way to do this is through planned progress monitoring.

PLANNED PROGRESS MONITORING

Add up all the programme bars in either days or person weeks, and create a cumulative line representing the planned progress. At regular intervals review the progress of each bar on the programme, add up the person days/weeks completed and compare this point to the planned position. Draw a horizontal line between the points and calculate how far you are ahead or behind programme, and take the appropriate action. See chart opposite.

This example of planned progress monitoring at week 10 shows that:

- The architectural elevations and envelope details are not complete.
- The floor plans showing the finishes are more complete than expected.
- The M+E drawings are not as finished as anticipated, which has resulted in the integration workshops being delayed.
- Because the details are not complete this has also had an impact on the production of a cost check at this stage.
- By projecting a horizontal line from the actual completed line until it intersects the projected line, the overall delay to the programme can be estimated at 1 week and 1 day.

DESIGN PROGRAMME
STAGE 4 PROGRAMME

SCENARIO D : NEW CENTRAL LIBRARY
ACTIVITY SCHEDULE

	Week No.	1	2	3	4	5	6	7	8	9	10	11	12	13	14	15	16	17	18	19	20
Activities per week		2.1	2.1	7	7.1	8.1	8.2	7	7.1	7.2	7.1	10	10.2	10.1	10.1	9.1	9.1	6.1	6.1	1	1
Cumulative activities		2.1	4.2	11.2	18.3	26.4	34.6	41.6	48.7	55.9	63.0	73.0	83.2	93.3	103.4	112.5	121.6	127.7	133.8	134.8	135.8
Rounded up		3	5	12	19	27	35	42	49	56	63	73	84	94	104	113	122	128	134	135	136
Cumulative activities completed		3	5	12	16	27	35	40	44	51	55										

Planned activities —
Actual —

Delay: 6 days

2.7
An example of planned progress
monitoring on a simple project.

WHO IS IN THE PROJECT TEAM AT STAGE 4?

The core project roles at Stage 4 include the client, project lead, lead designer, architect, civil and structural engineer, building services engineer, cost consultant, health and safety advisor, contract administrator and construction lead. Additional roles may include an acoustic consultant, archeologist, BREEAM assessor (to monitor the building's sustainability performance against the Building Research Establishment's Environmental Assessment Method), cladding specialist, catering consultant, access consultant, facilities management advisor, fire engineer, highways consultant, interior designer, landscape architect, lighting designer, party wall surveyor, security advisor, signage designer and sustainability advisor. For a description of these roles, refer to Figure 6.1 in the RIBA publication, Assembling a Collaborative Project Team.

By Stage 4 the roles of the project team members will be well established, although if the procurement route selected is design and build the architectural role may be split into two. Under this procurement route the initial design team can be retained to advise the client on the development of the project through to completion, whilst the contractor may bring their own design team – including an architect who is new to the project, who takes on the role of detailing the building and is referred to as the 'contractor's architect'.

THE CONTRACTOR'S ARCHITECT

The contractor's architect is a term used to describe the relationship of the architect and the contractor when working together on a design and build project. Under this relationship, the architect is employed directly by the contractor. They should be experts in delivery with a strong understanding of products and performance. They may be a new architect to the project or the initial architect novated to the contractor.

TAKING ON MULTIPLE ROLES

Beware of agreeing to undertake a novated role with the contractor and a separate appointment giving consultancy advice to the employer. The two roles may lead to a conflict of interest for the designer, who could be tasked with advising the contractor and the employer on the same point.

If the initial architect is to be novated to the contractor, the client may procure the services of a second architect to advise them during construction. Many of the roles may be undertaken by the same person, particularly on smaller projects where one might expect the architect to take on the roles of project leader, lead designer, architect and contract administrator. Their responsibilities during Stage 4 are described overleaf.

RESPONSIBILITIES DURING STAGE 4

Project lead:
- Ensure that the project is delivered to the programme.
- Develop a package strategy for the technical design drawings (management contract).
- Procure critical work packages (management contract).
- Manage change processes.
- Manage project implementation risks.
- Manage information flow between the parties.

Lead designer:
- Manage all aspects of the design.
- Coordinate the design development.
- Integrate the work of specialist subcontractors.
- Agree any necessary adjustments to the Design Responsibility Matrix.

Design team members:
- Develop the Technical Design.
- Provide sufficient information for regular cost checks.
- Ensure that statutory authority submissions are complete.
- Complete risk assessments of the building in use, construction and demolition.
- Review contractor proposals and methodology.
- Prepare tender recommendations (for traditional procurement and package procurement under a management contract).

Contract administrator:
- Administer the terms and conditions of the Building Contract (Stage 5).

How do you work out what resources are required at this stage?

The fee for this stage will generally have been agreed along with the Schedule of Services at Stage 1 Preparation and Brief. In some instances, such as design and build procurement, the design team may be appointed at this stage and be new to the project; alternatively, the existing design team may now know significantly more about the project than they did at Stage 1. In either case it will be appropriate to revisit the resource and fee plans for the project.

In order to confirm that you have the correct fee proposal for this stage, it is important that the fee is built up from the allocation of resources against an agreed schedule of deliverables. Start by scheduling out all the documents you need to produce for the stage. This includes all drawings, reports, schedules and specifications. Once the schedule of work has been identified, allocate a resource to complete that element of work. Historically, an allowance of somewhere between three and four person days per drawing has been the appropriate time to allow. However, this can be reduced through the use of BIM software by the whole team. This period, on average, allows sufficient time for design team meetings, design reviews, product selection and producing the drawing itself. Add further time for exceptional negotiations, production of specifications, procurement and any value-engineering work that it is anticipated will be required. If the project is being procured under a management contract, then also include some extra time for complex tender processes. The allocated resource should be costed and compared to the overall fee allocation. As a guide, the proposed fee should represent approximately 30% of the overall fee – although the chosen procurement route will have an impact on the overall distribution of fees, as will the complexity of the design solution and the schedule of services commissioned.

If the cost of the resources greatly exceeds 30% of the overall fee, then the team will need to review the level of detailed information that they have agreed to provide. If the cost of resources is substantially less than 30% of the overall fee, then it will be necessary to check that the schedule of deliverables is comprehensive.

The resource plan at Figure 2.8 (overleaf) shows:

- The overall size of the team required to complete the tasks.
- The number of drawings and schedules anticipated, based on three person days per drawing.
- The full resource cost for the stage including client liaison, meetings and workshops.

PROJECT TEAM RESOURCE PLAN
STAGE 4 PROGRAMME

SCENARIO D: NEW CENTRAL LIBRARY

ACTIVITY	DRWG NO.	ROLE	RATE PER HOUR	RATE PER DAY	MAN DAYS TOTAL
Management team					
Client liaison: meetings		Director	100.00	800.00	10.00
Integration workshops		Associate	75.00	600.00	13.00
General arrangements					
Architectural plans	20	Associate	75.00	600.00	12.00
		Architect	50.00	400.00	30.00
Architectural sections	10	Architect	50.00	400.00	22.00
		Architectural Assistant	40.00	320.00	30.00
Envelope					
Architectural elevations	6	Associate	75.00	600.00	15.00
		Architect	50.00	400.00	18.00
External envelope details	10	Architect	50.00	400.00	30.00
Roof details	8	Architectural Assistant	40.00	320.00	10.00
Floors					
Floor finishes plans	10	Architect	50.00	400.00	26.00
Floor details	5	Architectural Assistant	40.00	320.00	20.00
Walls					
Wall plan types	10	Architect	50.00	400.00	22.00
		Architectural Assistant	40.00	320.00	10.00
Wall details	7	Architectural Assistant	40.00	320.00	20.00
Ceilings					
Ceiling finishes plan	10	Architect	50.00	400.00	12.00
Ceiling details	5	Architectural Assistant	40.00	320.00	20.00
Specification					
Specifications		Associate	75.00	600.00	14.00
Schedules	3	Architect	50.00	400.00	18.00
		Architectural Assistant	40.00	320.00	20.00
STAGE 4 Information Exchange		Architect	50.00	400.00	10.00
Total	104				382.00

Resource check	Total man days
	Total resource

2.8
Illustration of an architectural team resource plan.

TECHNICAL DESIGN

1	2	3	4	5	6	7	8	9	10	11	12	13	14	15	16	17	18	19	20	Totals
1	1		1		1		1		1		1		1		1		1			8,000.00
1				1	2			3			2	1		2		1				7,800.00
2	2	2	2	2	2															7,200.00
5	5	5	5	5	5															12,000.00
5	5	3	3	3	3															8,800.00
5	5	5	5	5	5															9,600.00
		3	3	2	1	3	3													9,000.00
		2	2	2	2	5	5													7,200.00
		5	5	5	5	5	5													12,000.00
						5	5													3,200.00
						5	5	5	5	3	3									10,400.00
								5	5	5	5									6,400.00
								5	5	3	3	3	3							8,800.00
								5	5											3,200.00
										5	5	5	5							6,400.00
										2	2	2	2	2	2					4,800.00
												5	5	5	5					6,400.00
										5	3	3	3							8,400.00
												3	3	3	3	3	3			7,200.00
														5	5	5	5			6,400.00
																		5.00	5.00	4,000.00
																				157,200.00
19	18	25	26	25	26	23	24	23	21	23	24	22	22	17	16	9	9	5	5	
3.8	3.6	5	5.2	5	5.2	4.6	4.8	4.6	4.2	4.6	4.8	4.4	4.4	3.4	3.2	1.8	1.8	1	1	

How do you decide who does what?

In order to complete Technical Design, it is important that all the information required for the building to be constructed is developed – and, in particular, that all the interfaces between different specialist subcontractors have been considered and allocated to the appropriate designer.

The production of the Technical Design will generally be more efficient when the most appropriate person produces the information; this will ensure that it is only produced once. None the less, the architect will still need to convey the design intent that they have for the detail to the specialist designer. The Design Responsibility Matrix (DRM) can help to clarify this.

RIBA: DESIGN RESPONSIBILITY MATRIX INCORPORATING INFORMATION EXCHANGES
STAGE 4 PROGRAMME

SCENARIO B: SMALL-SCALE HOUSING DEVELOPMENT

| | | STAGE 4 TECHNICAL DESIGN | | |
| | ASPECT OF DESIGN | DESIGN TEAM | | |
Classification	Title	Design responsibility	Level of design	Information exchange
	Foundations	Structural Engineer	Full (proprietary)	1:100
	External walls	Architect	Full (proprietary)	1:50
	Render	Architect	Full (proprietary)	1:10
	Timber windows	Architect	Performance	1:20
20-25-75	Roof lights	Architect	Full (proprietary)	1:10
	Structural roof	Structural Engineer	Full (generic)	1:100
20-50-50	Metal sheet roof systems	Architect	Full (generic)	1:10
	Internal walls	Architect	Full (proprietary)	1:20
25-25-10	Balustrades and handrails	Architect	Full (generic)	1:10
25-50-20	External doors	Architect	Full (generic)	1:10
25-50-20	Internal doors and doorsets	Architect	Full (proprietary)	1:10
30-70-90	Tanking and damp proof membranes	Structural Engineer	Full (proprietary)	1:20
50-10-20	Below-ground pumped drainage systems	Mechanical Engineer	Full (proprietary)	1:20
75-75-50	Mechanical engineering services control and management systems	Mechanical Engineer	Performance	1:50

2.9
An extract from a typical
Design Responsibility Matrix.

DEMARCATION OF RESPONSIBILITIES

For example, the demarcation of responsibility for drainage in a building can often be contentious. The role of the civil engineer should extend to the top of the ground-floor slab, the services engineer should complete the drainage through the building to the appliances. The architect may be identified to complete the builder's work detailing through the roof and/or ground-floor slab; they may also be responsible for coordinating the work. If the roof is a specialist system and the drainage pipe penetrates this, then a specialist subcontractor could be best placed to detail the roof. Many of these responsibilities can be defined at Stage 1 when the Design Responsibility Matrix first comes into existence. At Stage 4 we are able to put these early decisions into practice.

STAGE 4 TECHNICAL DESIGN

	CONTRACTOR			
Design responsibility	Level of design	Information exchange	CDP	Notes
N/A			No	
N/A			No	Structural Engineer to provide structural integrity advice
N/A			No	
Contractor	Full (proprietary)	1:10	Yes	
N/A			No	
N/A			No	
N/A			No	
N/A			No	
Contractor	Full (proprietary)	1:10	Yes	Structural Engineer to provide loading calculations
N/A			No	
N/A			No	
N/A			No	Architect to consult on details and systems
N/A			No	
Contractor	Full (proprietary)	1:10	Yes	

The RIBA Plan of Work Tool Box, available online, gives an excellent template for the DRM, and should be used to monitor the activities to be carried out by each member of the design team. The matrix is completed at Stage 1, and whilst this example is not representative of all the elements on a project it provides sufficient examples to illustrate the content to be included.

From this worked example, reviewed at the outset of Stage 4, the following points can be observed:

- The external walls will be designed and detailed by the architect to a full, proprietary standard. Specific products will be selected and specified. The structural engineer is expected to provide a support role, supplying information on structural stability and movement joints.
- The windows will be specified as a performance item. This will enable the contractor to select a supplier who meets the performance standards specified.
- The metal-sheet roof systems will be designed to a full, generic standard. The full design will be complete, but the choice of the final product is left to the contractor.
- The following parties have a design responsibility:
    ~ Architect.
    ~ Structural engineer.
    ~ Mechanical engineer.
    ~ Contractor.

What happens if the contractor tables their own Design Responsibility Matrix?

Many contractors, particularly when they commission the design team to work for them under a design and build procurement route, have their own version of a Design Responsibility Matrix. Following the RIBA Plan of Work 2013 will ensure that the scope of work included in the fee will be fully captured in the DRM produced at Stage 1. As Stage 4 Technical Design commences, it will be possible to explain to the contractor what was included in the scope of work at the outset of the project and how their fee may be affected if the scope changes.

HOW DOES THE CHOICE OF PROCUREMENT
affect Stage 4?

During Stage 4 all design work is concluded, including that of the specialist subcontractors, so it is important that a methodology is put in place to procure the services of any contractor with design responsibilities. If design and build is the chosen procurement route, then tender action will have already taken place as part of Stage 3; however, if a more traditional approach is adopted then tender action will occur during Stage 4. This route could mean that all items are fully designed by the design team but that there still may be contractor-designed portions to complete. Often the portion of design left to complete is the detailing work or fabrication drawings undertaken by the specialist subcontractors. This design work should be approved by the design team and integrated with the main design information. The design team must make clear what the specialist subcontractor has to design and where the design responsibility lies.

FABRICATION DRAWINGS

A fabrication drawing shows a component that is to be made off site. It does not incorporate any further design work but merely takes an embedded component and clearly identifies its size, material and method of fabrication. The responsibility for the design of the system still rests with the design team.

What are the different procurement routes?

Although there are a number of different procurement routes incorporated in the RIBA Plan of Work 2013, they do not fundamentally affect what information has to be completed in order to get a project built. The different routes can, however, affect the timing of the stages and the responsibilities within the team.

Single-stage design and build

The ideal stage to go to tender for this procurement route is at the end of Stage 3 Developed Design. The advantage of tendering at this point is that the design team will have had sufficient time to develop the Developed Design, the detail of the project will be at a level that will enable the design team to produce detailed performance specifications, and the design brief for the project will be complete. This procurement route ensures that the contractors are directly engaged during Stage 4 Technical Design. It gives the opportunity for the contractor's architect to work directly with the building products and components that are to be used on the project, and in the process eliminates any drawing waste. Refer to Design: A Practical Guide to the RIBA Plan of Work 2013 Stages 2 and 3 for more detail.

Two-stage design and build

This route sometimes involves tendering at the end of Stage 2, as it gives the contractor an opportunity to engage with the design process before the Developed Design is complete. The contractor is selected on their approach to delivering the Concept Design, and in certain instances on their development of some of the early packages. Having been appointed to work with the design team throughout Stages 3 and 4, a contractor is not formally appointed until their final price for the works is agreed during Stage 4.

Management contracting

Under this procurement route the appointment of a management contractor provides the vehicle through which the building is procured via competitive package tenders. The advantage of this form of procurement is thought to be the speed with which the contractor can start work on site. There are a couple of points to be aware of that come with the benefit of speed.

The first point is that progressive fixity of the design is required. This can result in the Technical Design on the early packages, such as foundations and superstructure, being completed before the design of the envelope and interior is finalised. It can give rise to compromise in the later packages, as more and more constraints are put on the design team. For example: fixing the depths of structural beams before the accurate size of the mechanical plant is known may compromise the height of the ceilings.

The second point is that the client does not always know the full cost of the project when it starts on site. This is because the work for the foundations and superstructure may be let at a fixed price before the later packages have been tendered. In this case, only budget prices can be used to give the overall cost.

There are ways to minimise these risks. The contractor can be asked to own the risk. Each package can be open-book tendered to at least three contractors in order to ensure that a competitive price is obtained for the project. Time for integration and value engineering should be built into the progressive fixity programme in order to ensure that an effective design solution can be achieved.

This procurement route can also increase the amount of work that the design team have to complete, as the work is procured in separate tender clusters relating to the sequence of work (often referred to as packages). It is good practice at the time your fee is fixed to ensure that you limit the number of packages you may be asked to produce should management contracting be selected as the preferred procurement route.

For more information on management contracting, please refer to Design: A Practical Guide to the RIBA Plan of Work 2013 Stages 2 and 3 by Tim Bailey.

Traditional procurement

This is the most likely procurement route to be undertaken during Stage 4, and is often associated with smaller projects. Tendering for this procurement route takes place a considerable way through Technical Design. The exact timing will be dependent on how prescriptive the design team have been about the products and materials that are selected for the project. On simple buildings this could consist of all the materials, with nothing left for the contractor to select; in this case, tender action will occur towards the end of the stage. On more complex buildings, even though the overall procurement route is traditional there could still be some contractor's designed portion such as cladding. Leaving this to the contractor to source against a performance specification will ensure that best value is achieved for the client, the contractor takes full responsibility for programming and the design intent is satisfied. In this case the architect will have to revisit their technical drawings before completing Stage 4 to ensure that fully integrated technical drawings are developed prior to construction issue. It is recommended that only discrete aspects of the project are specified in this way.

CONTRACTOR'S DESIGNED PORTION (?)

The contractor's designed portion, or CDP, involves an agreement for the contractor to design specific parts of the works. Often, the portion of design left to the contractor is the detailing work undertaken by specialist subcontractors. CDP should not be confused with design and build contracts, where the contractor is appointed to design the whole of the works.

It is important contractually when using this procurement route to identify the products that you wish to use. This sets a prescriptive standard for the building. In some instances, where two or three suppliers may offer a similar product, alternative suppliers can be listed in the specification. Another way to allow the contractor to submit a competitive tender is to name the product but give the contractor the opportunity to suggest an alternative by including the words 'or similar approved' in the specification and on other information wherever those materials are mentioned. In any event, before starting the tender process it is important that the Developed Design has been translated into precise technical information in sufficient detail to allow for accurate pricing and for construction of the proposed works.

How do the different procurement routes affect the design team?

As soon as the procurement route has been determined, usually at Stage 1, the lead designer can complete their Design Programme. Each procurement route will give the design team access to the specialist subcontractors at different points throughout Stage 4. Under design and build the subcontractors will generally be engaged at the commencement of Stage 4, giving the design team access to definitive products and details. Under management contracting, the specialist subcontractors will be appointed throughout the stage as the technical design progresses. Under a traditional contract, the design team will not have access to the specialist subcontractors until towards the end of the stage. It is important that the resource plan and fee reflects this relationship. For example: on a complex project, with lots of specialist subcontractors engaged, the lead-designer role will involve more management and integration of information than on a relatively simple project, which may result in an increase in fees. To ensure that the full scope of the works is understood by all, it is good practice not only to identify in the specification those design items still to be completed but also to stipulate the deliverables expected from any of the specialist subcontractors.

Whatever the procurement route, the sequential activities described in the Plan of Work take place throughout the development of any project. However, the alternative procurement routes create different relationships between the design team, the client and the contractor. It is important to understand these relationships in order to define the different roles to be filled.

Under design and build procurement, the employer client will have already made a choice on the way to tackle Technical Design at this stage. They will either retain the design team to review the contractor's proposals, requesting the contractor to provide their own design team to complete Technical Design, or the employer client can novate the design team to the contractor. Whichever route the employer client selects, it is important that the contractor's architect establishes exactly what their duties are and how much work is required from the contractor. The following list gives some clarity to both roles under the design and build procurement route.

DEFINITION

Employer's design team:

- Review design development prepared by contractor's architect for compliance with employer's requirements.
- Attend dialogue workshops with contractor's design team.
- Advise client on opportunities for value engineering (VE), and attend VE workshops.
- Inspect finished work on behalf of the employer.
- If requested, administer the Building Contract.

Contractor's design team:

- Prepare contractor's proposals.
- Develop the Technical Design sufficient for construction.
- Together with the contractor's suppliers, develop a fully coordinated and integrated design solution.
- Review technical drawings produced by specialist suppliers for compliance with contractor's proposals.
- Prepare documentation for Building Control and other statutory approvals.
- Inspect finished work on behalf of the contractor.

Under a traditional contract, the design team are continuously engaged by the employer client. The architect may also be engaged to administer the terms of the Building Contract, taking on the role of contract administrator. During Stage 4, in addition to developing the Technical Design, there is a need to compile tender documentation, answer queries from the contractor during tender, review the contractor's proposals and make recommendations to the employer client on the appointment of a contractor.

Finally, under a management contract the design team are employed by the client but the development of the Technical Design will be programmed by the management contractor. The role of the design team will involve completing the Technical Design, in packages, to suit the contractor's programme.

A programme should be agreed that will enable the lead designer to complete a full integration exercise and bring Stage 4 to a conclusion.

Selecting the tenderers for a traditional contract at Stage 4

For public procurement an OJEU (Official Journal of the European Union) notice may need to be published, advertising the project and inviting potential contractors to tender. For private projects, a preliminary invitation to selected contractors will enable the project lead to decide whether they are interested and available to tender. In either case, the contractors should be selected from a fair comparison of capability. A list for such purposes may include:

- The financial standing of the company.
- The value of the project in comparison to the turnover and size of the contractor.
- The appropriate experience of the contractor and their team.
- The proposed methodology for building the project.
- The cost estimate for the works.
- The contractor's understanding of the project and its complexities.
- A recommendation from a third party or previous relationship.

What should be included in the tender set?

Tender documents should contain:

- Clear conditions for the submission, such as how many pages are required for each answer, so that all tenderers provide the same amount of information.
- Proposed timescales for the pre-construction and construction periods.
- All the technical information necessary to construct the project, including drawings, specifications and form of contract.
- The criteria that will be used to evaluate the contractors' submission.

Refer to the RIBA Job Book Ninth Edition for supplementary material on tendering and selecting a contractor.

Answering tender queries

It is important that all tenderers are treated equally during the tender period. Best practice is to collate all questions from the contractors, and publish all questions and answers simultaneously to all the tenderers. Unless there is an overriding complexity that is only identified during the tender period, it is best practice to avoid granting an extension of time.

Selecting a preferred contractor

As part of the evaluation process, the tender should be referred to the health and safety advisor for them to check the adequacy of allocated resources in respect of health and safety. The priced bills should be examined by the cost consultant, and the methodology and approach should be reviewed by the project lead and the design team. After all of the tenders have been evaluated, it may be appropriate to interview a shortlist from the most complete tender returns. An interview is an opportunity to meet the contractor's team and establish whether they fully understand the project that they are about to undertake. In many cases the contractor may have qualified their tender, and this also provides the opportunity to clarify and remove any qualifications. If the qualifications give the contractor an unfair advantage, then the tender should be rejected before it gets to this stage.

Unsuccessful tenderers should be notified as quickly as possible once the Building Contract has been let. A list of tenderers should be included, as should the percentage deviation from the winning tender.

SUMMARY

In this chapter we have looked at the technical information that needs to be produced in order to complete Stage 4. We have examined the use of a Design Programme and the role of the Design Responsibility Matrix. We have also looked at the impact of procurement on the design team during Stage 4. In the next chapter, we will consider:

- The key support tasks that need to be completed.
- The strategy documents, which require constant updating as the project develops.
- How to prepare for Building Control approval, and other approvals that may be required.
- What to expect at the Sustainability Checkpoints.
- How to prepare for the Information Exchange at the end of Stage 4.

CHAPTER 03

STAGE 4

TECHNICAL
DESIGN: PART 2

RIBA
Plan of
Work
2013

Stage 4

Technical Design

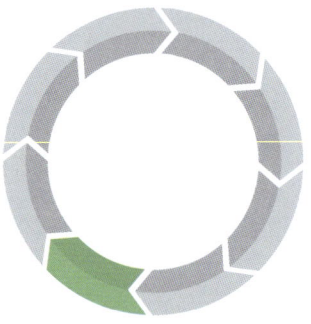

Task Bar	Tasks
Core Objectives	Prepare **Technical Design** in accordance with **Design Responsibility Matrix** and **Project Strategies** to include all architectural, structural and building services information, specialist subcontractor design and specifications, in accordance with **Design Programme**.
Procurement *Variable task bar*	*The Procurement activities during this stage will depend on the procurement route determined during Stage 1.*
Programme *Variable task bar*	*The RIBA Plan of Work 2013 enables this stage to overlap with a number of other stages depending on the selected procurement route.*
(Town) Planning *Variable task bar*	*The RIBA Plan of Work 2013 suggests that any conditions attached to a planning consent are addressed during this stage, prior to work starting on site during Stage 5.*
Suggested Key Support Tasks	Review and update **Sustainability, Maintenance and Operational** and **Handover Strategies** and **Risk Assessments**. Prepare and submit Building Regulations submission and any other third party submissions requiring consent. Review and update **Project Execution Plan**. Review **Construction Strategy**, including sequencing, and update **Health and Safety Strategy**. *A further review of the **Project Strategies** and documentation previously generated is required during this stage.*
Sustainability Checkpoints	• *Is the formal sustainability assessment substantially complete?* • *Have details been audited for airtightness and continuity of insulation?* • *Has the Building Regulations Part L submission been made and the design stage carbon/energy declaration been updated and the future climate impact assessment prepared?* • *Has a non-technical user guide been drafted and have the format and content of the Part L log book been agreed?* • *Has all outstanding design stage sustainability assessment information been submitted?* • *Are building **Handover Strategy** and monitoring technologies specified?* • *Have the implications of changes to the specification or design been reviewed against agreed sustainability criteria?* • *Has compliance of agreed sustainability criteria for contributions by specialist subcontractors been demonstrated?*
Information Exchanges (at stage completion)	Completed **Technical Design** of the project.
UK Government Information Exchanges	Not required.

OVERVIEW

This chapter will explain the tasks that need to be finished in order to complete Stage 4. In Chapter 2 we described how to get started on Stage 4, what level of information is to be prepared, how to develop a Design Programme and how to develop a Design Responsibility Matrix. Now we need to develop in detail the key support tasks that the project team will need to undertake. We will describe the review and update activities that have to be applied to all the strategies created in Stages 2 and 3. We will examine the more typical approvals that may be required at this stage, such as that required by Building Control. We will establish what needs to be done to ensure that the technical design underpins the Sustainability Strategy, and we will clarify what needs to be included in the Project Execution Plan and the Information Exchange.

WHAT ARE THE SUGGESTED KEY
support tasks for Stage 4?

The Suggested Key Support Task bar:

- Clarifies the activities required to achieve the Sustainability Aspirations, thus reducing the carbon emissions related to the building, and those required to embed BIM into the process.
- Sets out key tasks in relation to statutory requirements, such as those relating to Building Control submissions, project and design management protocols, and roles and responsibilities.
- Requires that the team is properly assembled, and that buildability, health and safety and other considerations and logistics are considered early in the process, by using the Project Execution Plan and Construction Strategy in the preparations.
- Calls for the Sustainability, Maintenance and Operational, and Handover Strategies to be reviewed and updated.
- Requires the Risk Assessments to be reviewed and updated.

Reviewing and updating the Project Strategies

As the project develops, a number of strategic documents are created to assist the project team in the design of the building. From the outset, at Stage 1, a Project Execution Plan (PEP) is prepared, which is updated at every stage through to Stage 5. As the Concept Design is developed at Stage 2, then the design team prepare a number of support documents to ensure that all aspects affecting the design are considered. These include: a Sustainability Strategy, a Maintenance and Operational Strategy, a Handover Strategy, a Construction Strategy and a Health and Safety Strategy. At Stage 4 these strategies, together with the PEP, need to be reviewed and updated.

Developing the Maintenance and Operational Strategy

The Maintenance and Operational Strategy developed during the Concept Design stage, and updated during the Developed Design stage, now needs to be reviewed and updated again in order to capture any additional detail that the specialist designers may contribute. This is the final review of the Maintenance and Operational Strategy, and it will form a key part of the documentation contained in the Information Exchange at the end of Stages 5 and 6.

Ensure that the following points have been considered at Stage 2, and update any gaps in the information:

- Eliminate hazards by developing Technical Design solutions that avoid foreseeable risks associated with cleaning and maintaining the building.
- Identify any specialist equipment that may be required to clean or maintain the building. Ensure that it can access the building, and that appropriate costs are captured in the project budget. For example, selecting a cherry picker to clean the elevations of an internal atrium will require a detailed study on access to the atrium, availability of the equipment (if hired) and the creation of a suitable storage area (if purchased) – see Figure 3.1.

3.1

A cherry picker designed to enter through standard double doors at the SELF Hotel, Hamburg.

- Provide adequate information to the health and safety advisor relating to any uncommon or significant risk associated with maintaining the building.
- Clarify maintenance frequencies with the specialist suppliers and input the data into the life-cycle cost analysis for the project. For example, to preserve the warranty on an external metal roof finish, it may be necessary to wash it down regularly; if the methodology for achieving this has not been considered at Stage 2, then the selection of an economical initial product may turn into a long-term cost liability.

To get the most out of the building in use, it will be important to explain to the owner how to operate the building to achieve the optimum performance. The operational strategy should include the following:

- Performance targets and anticipated outcomes for energy consumption.
- Any technical assumptions that may affect the performance of the building.
- Planned maintenance requirements for the building components and equipment, including methodologies for safe working.
- The life expectancy of significant building components.

If the Technical Design has been prepared using BIM, then some of this information, such as life expectancy, can be attached to the individual systems and components within the model. It may also be necessary on some projects to generate an indicative running cost from the Maintenance and Operational Strategy so that the client has a full understanding of the ongoing costs associated with the design.

Updating the Health and Safety Strategy

By the time we move into Stage 4, the Health and Safety Strategy will have been carefully considered. The main items to update will include the residual risks carried forward from Stage 3, together with any developments in the construction methodology now that the contractor is able to fully engage with buildability.

The residual hazards carried forward from Stage 3 need to be eliminated as Technical Design progresses. The design risk register is a 'live' document that is commenced at Concept Design stage and is reviewed at all stages as the design develops. It will describe the significant or unusual risks associated with the construction, future use, cleaning, maintenance and demolition of the building. With the specialist subcontractors now appointed, an opportunity

SCENARIO A: RISK REGISTER FOR A SMALL HOUSE EXTENSION

Description	Hazard: the potential to cause harm	Persons at risk	Event: an event causing harm as a result of the hazard	Can the risk be eliminated? YES/NO	Design mitigation measures taken	**RESIDUAL RISK** Required controls by others in construction/ use/maintenance/ cleaning/demolition
Opening up existing building	Damage to existing structure, risk of cracking or collapse if inadequately supported	Occupants, contractors	Potential collapse of existing structure if inadequately supported	Yes	Ensure structural calculations are approved for all permanent and temporary support. Survey existing facilities to identify any existing damage before work commences	Contractor to provide method statement prior to demolition. Provide adequate support to existing structure
Underground services	Damage to existing services	Contractors	Damage to HV cable on excavation	Yes	Survey existing ground to identify location of services. Examine record drawings and consult Utility providers	Hand dig if known obstructions are present
Existing site condition	Unknown hazards	Contractors	Unknown event	Yes	Detailed information on ground conditions to be obtained before work commences	
Children	Entering the site uninvited by children and other family members	Family members	Injury caused by a lack of understanding of building hazards	Yes	Project team to induct the family into the dangers of a live building site	Contractor to ensure site is safe and secure from the family accommodation each evening
Roof terrace	Exposed finish to roof	Contractor, client	Paved walking surface may become hazardous in wet or freezing conditions. Small gaps between paviours may be hazardous to client wearing sharp heeled shoes	No	N/A	Contractor to ensure all elements of balustrading/ latchway are installed and fully commissioned before handover
Polymeric membrane roof covering	Slips on wet surfaces	Contractors	Polymeric roof covering is designated as having a high slip potential when wet	No	Design team to consider access routes and frequency as part of the detailed design phase. Produce selection to minimise maintenance access requirements	Roof covering and pavers to be scrubbed and swept of mould/debris build-up at least once a year. Roof access must not be granted in frosty, windy or wet conditions
Internal courtyard window cleaning	Cleaning of first floor windows could result in a fall	Client	Client falling and causing injury or death	No	Windows to be fixed or open in for cleaning. Latchway point adjacent to opening	Due to restricted access, windows to the first floor can be cleaned with a telescopic squeegee (Tucker® Pole system, 14m pole) and de-ionised water
Roof finishes	Falls from height	Contractors		No	N/A	Contractor to ensure all elements of balustrading/ latchway are installed and fully commissioned before handover. Special edge protection to prevent workers falling during construction
Lobby balustrade	On-site drilling	Contractors	HAVS; noise from hammer-drilling; injury from flying debris	No	Cast-in fixings not practicable; however drilled fixings arranged to enable use of drilling rig to eliminate HAVS exposure	Contractor to ensure safe method of working

3.2

Extract taken from a completed design risk register for a small house extension.

arises to establish if the Technical Design has had an impact on the residual risks carried forward from Stage 3. A good way to evaluate this is to hold a risk workshop with the project team, including the health and safety advisor. The workshop can discuss in detail the identified risks and the mitigation factors that have been developed to reduce their impact. Record the outcome of the workshop on the final iteration of the design risk register (see Figure 3.2). There may be some residual risks that only the principal contractor can mitigate. This is also an opportunity to discuss these with the contractor, and ensure that they fully understand them before construction commences.

Developing the Handover Strategy

At this stage, the Handover Strategy should include provision for the following:

- A commissioning programme including details of all handover dates.
- Commissioning periods.
- Any specialist installations that may be required.
- Furniture installation periods.
- Equipment installations and connections.
- Cleaning services.
- Health and safety inspection.
- Final snagging and defect-resolution programme.

Any phased or sectional handover must be identified on the programme, and work put in hand to ensure that the building operates adequately and safely throughout the phased handover.

Refer to Chapter 4, Stage 5 Construction, for detailed requirements at handover and the procedures to be adopted.

UPDATING THE HANDOVER STRATEGY

The project team will need to contribute to the finalisation of the Handover Strategy. The services engineer will need to confirm commissioning periods once the final equipment has been selected. Programme periods and installation dates will be agreed with the contractor, the client and the lead designer once all the products have been finalised. It is the responsibility of the lead designer at Stage 4 to ensure that all the contributions of the team are collated into one strategic document.

Developing the Construction Strategy document with the contractor

The Construction Strategy will consider specific aspects of the approach to building the project. It will need to address the following topics:

- How the site is laid out, vehicular and pedestrian access (including safe routes for pedestrians).
- Where materials will be stored, particularly delicate or dangerous materials.
- Crane locations, both fixed tower cranes and working zones for mobile cranes.
- How materials are intended to be delivered to the site.
- How preassembly and prefabricated components are to be used on the project.
- Safe working practices, including permission-to-work permits.
- Disposal of waste, and any recycling plans.

It should also highlight for the contractor what is expected of them at handover (Stage 6), how the building is anticipated to perform in use (Stage 7) and what their responsibilities will be post-Practical Completion.

Updating the Project Execution Plan

In addition to the individual strategies for construction, maintenance and operation, and handover, the team will need to review and update the Project Execution Plan (PEP). A comprehensive PEP at Stage 4 will include the following:

1. **Project Objectives and Priorities**
   - Project particulars, including the client's name, the project name, details of any approved business case.
   - Objectives of the project and desired outcomes.
   - Approvals and consents.
   - Approved budget and programme.
   - Location, physical environment and design constraints.
2. **Project Risk Management**
   - Highlight critical issues, risk and uncertainties, which could threaten achievement of the project objectives.
   - Detail the procedures for mitigating risk.

3. **Organisation Roles and Responsibilities**
   - ~ Describe the project organisation, including:
     - o The names, addresses, telephone numbers and contact details of all organisations involved in the project.
     - o Their roles and relationships with each other.
     - o Their responsibilities and the authority delegated to them.

4. **Design Management**
   - ~ Set out how the project will be managed and controlled in terms of design.
   - ~ Design deliverables and milestones.
   - ~ Safety checks.
   - ~ Control of change to designs.
   - ~ Arrangement for design reviews.
   - ~ Coordination responsibilities.
   - ~ Planning permission.
   - ~ Evaluation and approvals.

5. **Project Controls**
   - ~ Change management.
   - ~ Programme management.
   - ~ Work element breakdown to define scope and resources, key decision dates and risk items.
   - ~ Cost management.
   - ~ Quality control.

WHAT APPROVALS ARE REQUIRED AT THIS STAGE?

In addition to planning permission, submitted at Stage 2 or 3, the main statutory approval that will be required in the UK is Building Regulation approval. This can be sought from either the Building Control department of the local authority or from an approved inspector. In England and Wales there are 14 Approved Documents that give general guidance on how to comply with the Building Regulations. Each document deals with individual aspects of the technical design of a building. Their principal purpose is to ensure the health and safety of people in and around all types of buildings – domestic, commercial and industrial. A full list of the Approved Documents is below:

- **Part A:** Structural integrity.
- **Part B:** Fire protection, compartmentation and life-safety measures.
- **Part C:** Site preparation and resistance to contaminants and moisture.
- **Part D:** Toxic substances.
- **Part E:** Resistance to the passage of sound.
- **Part F:** Ventilation.
- **Part G:** Sanitation, hygiene and water efficiency.
- **Part H:** Drainage and water disposal.
- **Part J:** Combustion appliances and fuel-storage systems.
- **Part K:** Protection from falling, collision and impact.
- **Part L:** Conservation of fuel and power.
- **Part M:** Access to and use of buildings.
- **Part N:** Glazing.
- **Part P:** Electrical safety – dwellings.

Approval is obtained by submitting the Technical Design information to the approved inspector so that they can check the information for compliance. Remember, the Approved Documents illustrate a method for achieving compliance with the regulations, but there are also alternative approaches that can achieve the same effect.

AN EXAMPLE OF AN ALTERNATIVE APPROACH TO USING APPROVED DOCUMENT B ON A LARGE PROJECT

For the successful operation of a major assembly building like an airport terminal, it may not be possible to achieve the compartment sizes specified in the Building Regulations Approved Document B. By adopting a fire-engineering approach, the extra size of the compartments may be offset by other safety measures such as fire suppression, reduced fire load and/or enhanced evacuation provisions.

In addition to Building Control, there may be additional approvals that the project requires at Stage 4. A typical checklist should include the following:

- **Party-wall agreement:** Where a wall is shared between neighbours and an agreement needs to be reached with the adjoining owners, the project may be subject to the Party Wall Act 1996.
- **Licensing:** A premises licence will be required if it is intended to do any of the following in the new building: sell alcohol; serve hot food between certain hours of the day; or put on a theatrical performance, film, indoor sporting event, live or recorded music or dancing facilities.
- **Statutory obligations applying to all services crossing or supplying the site:** For most services – eg water, gas and electricity – building owners, and particularly domestic premises, have a right to receive a supply although they may have to reach an agreement with the service supplier on the cost of that supply.
- **Tree Preservation Orders (TPOs):** These will have been dealt with at the planning stage.
- **Rights to light:** These will have been dealt with at the planning stage.
- **Environmental impacts that may affect the development:** These will have been dealt with at the planning stage.
- **Other restrictions on the building, such as listed or ancient monument status:** If the building is listed, then consent will be required for all works that involve demolition, alteration or extension. This is generally submitted along with the planning application, but it may require ongoing approval dependent on the nature and detail of the works.

WHAT OTHER TASKS ARE REQUIRED AT THIS STAGE?

There are a number of additional activities and processes that will help the project team towards a successful outcome to Stage 4. They will need to ensure that changes to the design are kept to a minimum, and that a change control process is in place to facilitate this. All the work of the specialist sub-consultants will need to be checked and reviewed before integrating their information into the final Technical Design. The final opportunity for value engineering the design arises once the contractor and specialist subcontractors are all appointed.

Dealing with change and Change Control Procedures

Before the start of Stage 4, the Stage 3 Developed Design must be approved by the client to avoid unnecessary waste in the production of the Technical Design. To ensure that the design team are not thrown off course during Stage 4, the Change Control Procedure put in place at the commencement of Stage 3 should be adopted. Any additional work generated by the client or suggested by the contractor should be fully analysed, and impacts on time and cost explained to the client before the new work is instructed.

WHY IS CHANGE CONTROL IMPORTANT?

A variety of factors can generate change on a project. They should all be documented, and the project team should take a view on their impact on time and money. By way of example: the purchaser of one of the five new homes being built by the residential developer in Scenario B wishes to convert one of the bathrooms into a wet room for disabled use. As this was not part of the original brief, the design team will need to estimate how much information is affected and what amount of time will be required to change it. Having received this information from the team, the developer can add the design team's cost to the change of specification cost and the cost of removing the existing bathroom. The developer can then decide whether to absorb those costs in the interests of a sale, pass them on to the purchaser for approval or refuse the sale if the costs are prohibitive. It is important that the design team don't start the change until a signed instruction has been given from their employer.

Checking and reviewing the Technical Design

Prior to sharing the Technical Design with the other members of the design team, or before issuing it to the contractor for construction, it is important to check and review the information for accuracy and completeness. This is best done by a review team that comprises all members of the project team.

If the design has been developed using BIM, then there are a number of clash-detection software applications that will enable the review team to identify areas where the information is not fully coordinated. Another technique is for the review team to take a virtual tour through the model to identify obvious clashes or irregularities. In parallel with checking that the information is coordinated, it is also important to review the technical design for content and accuracy. This can be achieved in a number of ways:

- **A peer review:** An independent professional of the same discipline can review the documentation and prepare a report highlighting any areas of concern.

- **A technical design review:** The project team present the information to an invited panel of experts. The panel can interrogate the completeness of the information and offer development suggestions from their own experience.
- **A desktop review:** This may be conducted by the project leader or a senior member of the project team. They can check the work in progress for technical content as well as checking the format of the data.
- **Self-checking:** This is a good discipline to adopt. Each individual producing the information takes time out at the start of each day to review their own work for accuracy.

Depending on the size of the project, it may be appropriate to deploy all or just a selection of the above methods. Whichever is/are adopted, it is good practice to record who the information was reviewed by at the time of the review.

Approval status of Technical Design information

The lead designer is responsible for checking the Technical Design information from the other designers, including the design team and any specialist designers, and ensuring that the design information forms a unified set of information for the contractor. In principle, the lead designer will check for dimensional fit, with the content of the information being checked beforehand by the individual discipline. It is good practice to adopt the following status on the information of others as it is reviewed.

- **A:** Approved, no further comments.
- **B:** Approved subject to the minor amendments marked on the drawings.
- **C:** Not approved; please amend the information and resubmit for approval.
- **D:** For information only; noted, but not certified by the reviewer.

In this way, the Technical Design can be developed in an iterative manner to ensure progress through the stage.

What is the impact of data and digital models on the checking process?

When working in a BIM environment, it is important that each member of the project team retain ownership and take responsibility for the information they produce. The roles and responsibilities of each team member will be described in the Design Responsibility Matrix. Protocols for uploading data, the status of information and access rights will be recorded in the BIM execution plan created at Stage 2 and updated as more members join the project team. Responsibility for coordination of the information should rest with all members of the project team under the stewardship of the project leader. Responsibility for the content of the information should remain with the team discipline producing it. Once these protocols are agreed and understood, the information can be interrogated either by using a variety of software packages or utilising some of the checking techniques described previously.

Approving materials and suppliers

As Technical Design progresses it will be necessary to identify all the materials on the project and the best source of supply. The project team will need to answer a number of questions when selecting appropriate materials:

- **Innovative materials:** What is the client's view of the use of innovative materials? Is there time to test new materials before they are used on the project? Do the materials give significant advantages – thermal, environmental, etc. – that cannot be achieved by tried and tested products?
- **Sustainability:** Do the chosen materials possess any sustainable characteristics? Will they contribute to the environmental credentials of the project during manufacture and construction, and during the life of the building? Can they be disposed of sensibly when the building is demolished?
- **Cost:** Are the preferred materials in budget, both as a capital cost and as a life-cycle cost?
- **Performance:** Do the chosen materials have the correct performance criteria? Are they suitably durable?
- **Certification:** Can the materials demonstrate performance through an Agrément Certificate or other recognised accreditation?

- **Availability:** Are the materials readily available? Can potentially long lead times be accommodated in the Construction Programme? Are they locally sourced or are they transported from afar?

In addition to making the final selection of materials, it will be necessary to ensure that the supplier can meet the needs of the project. A simple checklist to cover this would include production capacity, financial standing, reliability and experience. Once the project team have made their recommendations on materials and suppliers, it is important to discuss these with the client before final selection and placing orders.

The example of a system selection matrix at Figure 3.3 shows:

- That each attribute of the system is evaluated and scored by the project team in a workshop where different attributes can be debated.
- A weighting that can be applied to each attribute to raise the impact of certain features.
- That the cost of the product plays an important part, but is not the only determining factor.
- How it is possible to compare a wide variety of different systems on both subjective and objective criteria without simply deferring to capital cost.

Test certificates and testing specified products

These are a good way of understanding the performance of a product, but care should always be exercised when reviewing established test documentation. In many cases the condition created in the test may not be replicated in the project under way. In these circumstances, it may be necessary to call for a specific test of the material as it is to be used on the project. The test regime should be identified in the specification documentation so that the contractor has an opportunity to include the price in their construction cost. It is commonplace for members of the project team to witness such testing to ensure that the product passes, and this should be incorporated into the design fee for the project.

SYSTEM SELECTION MATRIX

LOCATION (insert room location here)	CRITERIA (this list to be populated from specifications)	OPTIONS							
	(Workshop to evaluate categories and weightings)	Access installation		Access maintain		Buildability		Visual appearance	
ELEMENT	Weight 1-10	5		3		6		8	
	Weight %	11.9		7.1		14.3		19.0	
CEILING	Metal acoustic	10	119	10	71	10	143	10	191
	Plasterboard	3	36	2	14	5	71	5	95
	Mineral fibre	2	24*	3	21	4	57	3	57
WALL FINISHES	Metal panels								
	Laminate panels								
	Ceramic tiles								
WALLS	Blockwork								
	Metal stud partition								
DOORS	Steel faced								
	Laminate faced								
	Painted								
FRAMES	Steel								
	Hardwood								
	Softwood painted								
SKIRTING	Integral								
	Timber								
	Tile								

* Score the product and multiply by the percentage

† Weight the characteristic of the material in order of importance

§ Multiply the subtotal by the cost factor to evaluate the products

Cleaning		Durability		Environ. perform.		Any other characteristics		SUBTOTAL	Cost rate per m²	Cost factor 1/rate x 100	Subtotal x cost factor
4		8		8†				42			
9.5		19.0		19.0				100			
10	95.238	10	190.476	8	152.381			962	67	1.5	1435.7
3	28.571	4	76.190	4	76.190			398	30	3.3	1325.4
1	9.524	1	19.048	3	57.143			245	45	2.2	545.0§

3.3
An example of a system selection matrix.

Completing the project information

In addition to the drawn information, the project information should include specifications and schedules to enable the contractor to accurately price and order the materials for the building.

SPECIFICATION WRITING

A well-written specification, when prepared in parallel with the drawn information, provides the proper balance between statutory, technical and aesthetic requirements. It should be written with clarity, be consistent and accurate, avoid repetition and the use of irrelevant clauses, and follow a recognised logic. There are a number of standard templates available, such as NBS Create, which not only provide an electronic template for editing purposes but are also capable of being linked to a digital model.

In principle, there are two types of specification:

- **Specifying by performance:** This is where specific products are not selected but a performance criterion is established that enables the contractor to select an acceptable product. It often relies on referencing established standards or codes of practice in order to define the minimum standard to be achieved. In this type of specification, there is a greater requirement than usual to verify that the quality of the product selected by the contractor meets the performance criteria. This may involve samples, testing and the provision of mock-ups, which can often be cost-prohibitive on a small project. None the less, it is an accepted way of specifying readily available products such as aluminium windows, demountable partitions and suspended ceilings, and is the best way to specify a bespoke cladding system.
- **A prescriptive specification:** The prescriptive approach is where the product and standards of workmanship are set out and defined in detail. With this type of specification it is possible to nominate a particular brand or range of acceptable brands, to ensure that the anticipated level of quality of product is achieved. This can be supplemented by specific execution clauses that define the tolerances, workmanship and quality levels that must be achieved in the installation.

In order to make the specification easy to use, and to encourage the construction team to refer to it readily alongside the drawn information, it is useful if it is laid out in a consistent manner. Each section of the specification should contain compliance, product and execution requirements. The compliance section can deal with testing, inspections, samples, mock-ups, submissions and approvals. It can also be an opportunity to review which items are contractor's designed portions and whether substitutions for branded products will be considered. The product section will describe all the building material to be used, including the finish, manufacturing tolerances and any performance criteria that the product itself should reach. The execution clauses will deal with the workmanship requirements.

Try to avoid embedding inspection or provision-of-sample clauses in the product and execution sections, as they can often be missed by the construction team.

SCHEDULES

Schedules are used to describe different conditions that apply to related items such as doors, windows or room finishes. They are a simple way of describing the subtle variations that may occur with these related items. As an example, doors may have a vision panel, a ventilation grille, a fire rating, wood or metal frames and differing relationships with the adjacent walls. These variations are best captured on a schedule to avoid redundant or excessive drawing. As the use of BIM becomes more prevalent, these schedules will be generated by the digital model.

WHAT TO DO IF THE PROJECT EXCEEDS

the target budget at this stage

Although the design will have been on budget at the end of Stage 3 it is possible that, with the development of specific details and the clarity of workmanship and material specifications required at this stage, the project starts to exceed the target budget. There are a number of processes to ensure this does not happen:

- Obtain an elemental project estimate from the cost consultant at the end of Stage 3. Interrogate it before technical detailing starts to make sure that the requirements of the design have been costed.
- As Technical Design develops, request regular reviews with the cost consultant.
- Insert material costs into the BIM model so that changes in quantities are accurately recorded.
- Market-test material costs with appropriate suppliers. Ensure that you get workmanship and delivery costs from the suppliers consulted.
- Undertake value-engineering workshops with the design team and contractor throughout the stage.

What is value engineering?

The purpose of value engineering (VE) is to ensure best value for your employer client without changing the quality of the approved design. It is a process that can enhance the outcome of a building; where possible it should be undertaken with the contractor once a preferred bidder has been selected, but before the contract has been let. In practice, the different procurement routes have an impact on the outcome of value engineering. With design and build procurement, for instance, there is a danger that the client may not see all of the savings generated by the VE exercise. This is because the saving created by an alternative product may not be offered in full to the client once the contract has been let.

Value engineering is also an opportunity for the contractor to improve the buildability of the proposed design – a feature that can influence construction costs. It is an opportunity for them to really offer their construction expertise to the design team. It is not to be confused with cost cutting, whereby alternative, inferior products and solutions are put forward in order to reduce the cost of the building.

The design team should be responsible for evaluating alternative solutions, and in order to ensure transparency a scoring matrix is a good way to appraise these. Real savings can often be made by understanding the full impact of a particular solution: Where is the material coming from? Can transport costs be reduced if the material is procured locally? Is there a more efficient module that will remove waste from the fabrication process? This type of added value results from the designers understanding the manufacturing process and 'designing for manufacture'. It requires an openness and transparency from the supply chain – in particular, the second-tier suppliers.

SCENARIO D: NEW CENTRAL LIBRARY FOR A SMALL UNITARY AUTHORITY

In the case of the new central library building, the design team wanted to examine the most cost-effective way of procuring the glazed cladding for the building. Two solutions were examined in detail:

- Option A: Glazing mullions at 1.8m centres.
- Option B: Glazing mullions at 2.5m centres.

When the team evaluated both proposals with the specialist subcontractor, the following was considered:

- The optimum size of the unitised cladding for transportation from Austria, the location of the fabricator: 1.8m panels could be double stacked on a transporter, and were therefore more economical.
- The optimum size of panel for cutting the glass panes: 1.8m panels produced the least waste.
- The integration of the cladding with the openings in the facade: 2.5m modules were a perfect match for the dimensions of the main entrances through the facade, and avoided trimming the opening with secondary steel.
- The speed of erection of the different panels: 2.5m panels had fewer lifts, less fixings and could be installed quicker.
- The visual appearance of both solutions.

The overall decision was to adopt option B, saving the client £55k whilst providing better coordination and improved visual appearance (see Figure 3.4).

When value engineering is used well, it can derive maximum value without compromising the quality of the design.

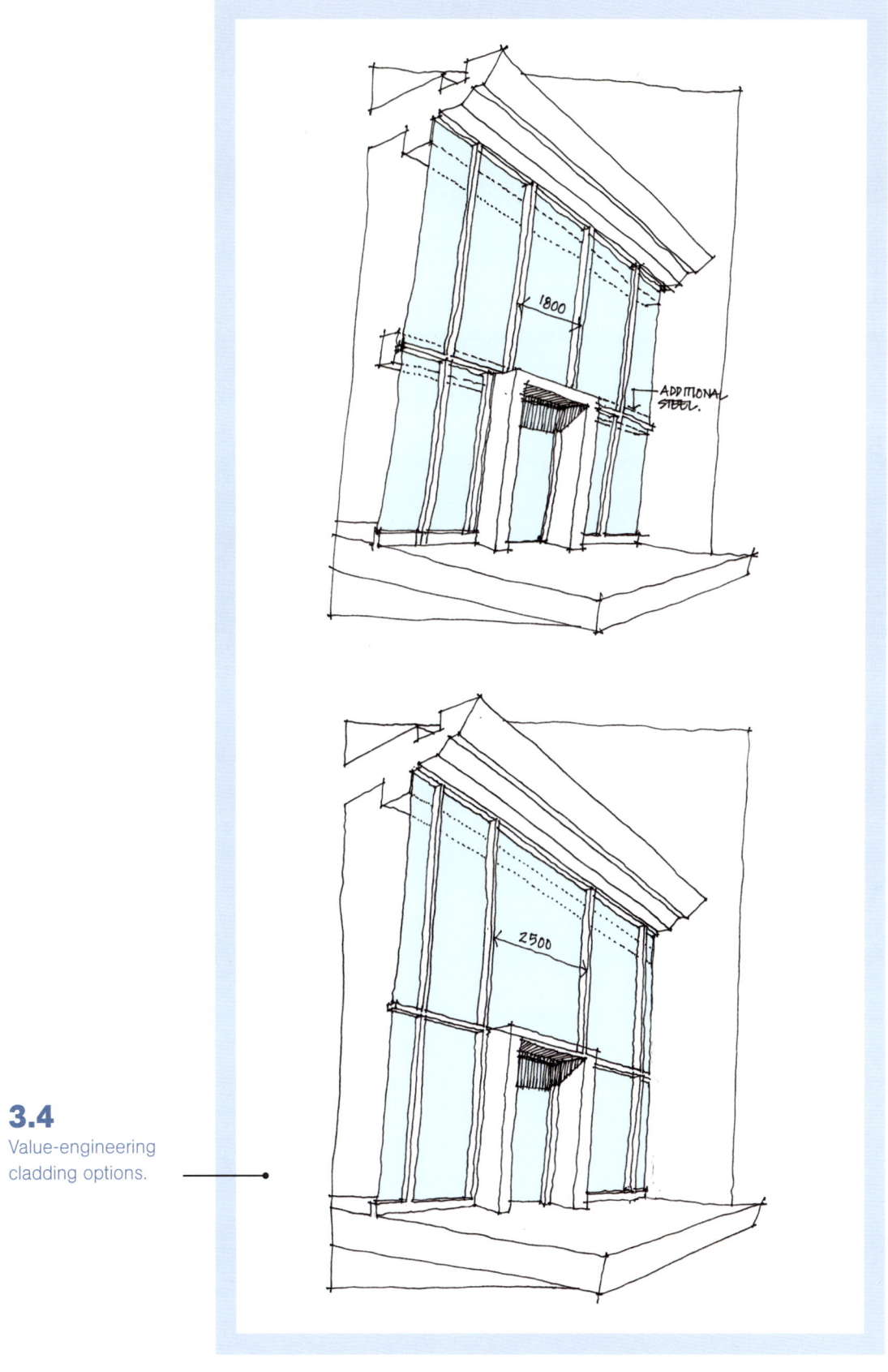

3.4
Value-engineering
cladding options.

SUSTAINABILITY CHECKPOINT 4:
Saving energy

As the Technical Design develops, it is important that it underpins the Sustainability Strategy. There are a number of key things to consider at this stage:

Checking details for airtightness and insulation

Review the project details for continuity of insulation and potential weak spots for air infiltration. If a detail raises particular concerns, it may be appropriate to simulate its performance in a computer model. If this is inconclusive, a test in laboratory conditions will enable a complete record of performance. It should be recognised, however, that conditions in a production plant – or, indeed, on the construction site itself – may not be as accurate as the laboratory, and allowances should be made.

Reviewing the design for impact on the Sustainability Strategy

There are a number of things to watch out for at this stage. Design subcontractors will need to be inducted into the Sustainability Aspirations of the project. Final material selection will need to be reviewed to ensure that it doesn't impact on any earlier assessments of the building's performance. The overall energy consumption of the building can now be checked against the assumptions made in earlier stages.

Preparing the Part L submission

As part of the Building Control submission, there is a requirement to demonstrate that the building will meet or exceed the energy standards outlined in Approved Document Part L. There are different criteria for different types of building, but in general there is a requirement to calculate the target emission rate for the building; the calculated CO_2 emission rate from the building as designed; and the specified performance levels that the building fabric, hot-water and fixed lighting systems are intended to reach. Passive control measures should be clarified, to ensure that there is no significant solar gain. Renewable energy sources, which are regularly a condition of planning approval, should also be identified and checked to ensure that they meet the planned performance.

WHAT NEEDS TO BE INCLUDED
in the Information Exchange?

At the end of Stage 4, there is an Information Exchange wherein the Technical Design information is handed over to the contractor. Included in this information should be the following:

- Complete technical design information, including:
    - ~ General-arrangement drawings.
    - ~ Drawn information describing the full scope of the works.
    - ~ Details showing principal interfaces.
    - ~ Specialist subcontractor design drawings.
    - ~ All technical specifications.
    - ~ Schedules describing all components.
- The Health and Safety Strategy, including the risk register.
- The Maintenance and Operational Strategy.
- The Handover Strategy.
- The Sustainability Strategy.
- All approvals received, and any still outstanding that may have to wait for the building to be inspected on completion.
- Updated cost information.
- Protocols on who owns and has access to information.
- How the information is to be retained, updated and superseded.
- The status of hard copies, digital copies and digital approvals.
- A list of specific software used in the creation of the data. Note: as specialist designers come on board, they will introduce new software products; it is important that the team ensure that non-exchangeable data types are not used.

The concept of an Information Exchange seems to imply relinquishing ownership of the information. This is not the case. The project team will always own their data throughout the project. It may be, however, that during the life of a project the overall leader of the project changes hands from the 'project lead' to 'construction lead' to 'client'. This 'baton-passing' generally occurs between Stage 4 and Stage 5 for project lead to contractor lead, and between Stage 5 and Stage 6 for contractor lead to client lead.

Final production of Technical Design 'for construction' status

Once the contractor is selected, the information is completed with the fabrication suppliers and a final set of fully integrated information is prepared. When this is issued to the contractor at the end of Stage 4, the designation of the information should change from Technical Design to 'for construction' status. This ensures that the contractor understands that the information is complete and ready for construction, that mistakes are avoided which can result from building to design information that is not coordinated or integrated, and that the responsibility for construction documentation rests with the design team.

SUMMARY

In this chapter, we have examined what tasks need to be done in order to bring Stage 4 to a conclusion. We have looked at what needs to be updated in the Project Strategies. We have catalogued the approvals that are still required at this stage, and described the differences between a performance and a prescriptive specification. As the Technical Design progresses, and specialist subcontractors become fully engaged in the process, we have illustrated methods that can be used to review their information and select the most appropriate materials. We have considered the impact of value engineering and what needs to be included in the Information Exchanges. In the next chapter, we will see how this information is used by the construction team.

A

Small residential extension for a growing family

SCENARIO SUMMARIES

WHAT HAS HAPPENED TO OUR PROJECTS BY THE END OF STAGE 4?

The design team including the architect, a structural engineer and the newly appointed mechanical engineer are producing Stage 4 information in isolation based on the Stage 3 co-ordinated deisgn. The architect, in the role of lead designer resolves interfaces and queries with the design team as they arise and as project lead, reviews the design responsibility matrix developed at Stage 1. They are able to use this to demonstrate to the client that a number of M&E items can be designed by the M&E engineer or a specialist subcontractor. The project team conclude that local contractors find it difficult to complete the final mechanical and engineering design because none of them has done this kind of thing before. It is agreed that the M&E engineer will do this work. The architect also points out that this also reduces the possible knock on impact during construction which may require further changes and costs.

A Building Regulation submission is prepared by the team including energy checks for Part L. The design team prepare the complete Technical Design for local contractors to price. All the products for the extension are selected by the design team working closely with the client. All the details are developed in 2D as agreed during Stage 3. Drawings are reviewed by the architect using drawing overlays.

Contract documents are prepared, and the architect uses these to explain to the contractor that the family will be living in the existing house whilst it is being extended, that safety will be paramount and that noisy activities may only be carried out between 10am and 4pm. The architect, in the role of contract administrator, explains to the client that the construction site will be under the control of the contractor and that the client must inform the contractor when he wishes to visit.

Development of five new homes for a small residential developer

Refurbishment of a teaching and support building for a university

The design team prepare technical design and specifications. All the products are selected by the design team working closely with the client. Many of the details are developed utilising generic details previously agreed with the developer. The design team must ensure that they are compliant with current legislation. The items covered by provisional sums at Stage 3 are now detailed and included in the tender documentation.

Following tender returns from three different contractors, the design team review all tenders and make a recommendation to the client on the preferred contractor. The contract administrator agrees the final tender price and obtains client approval to proceed.

The design team have been novated to the design and build contractor. They explain to the university client the change in their contractual relationship, and agree their scope of services with the contractor. The Design Responsibility Matrix clarifies all responsibilities, and a Design Programme is agreed for the production of the Technical Design. The contractor introduces the specialist subcontractors that he proposes to use.

As the Technical Design is completed, the architect, as lead designer, ensures that the design of the specialist subcontractors is integrated into the final design.

The design team advise the contractor of any areas of the existing building that may need opening up in order to complete the Technical Design.

The risk register is completed by the design team along with the health and safety advisor. A risk workshop is held to identify mitigation measures for any residual risks.

Working for a design and build contractor can cause problems for a novated team, ie they have a new client, but the old client may still expect a service from them that they cannot give. Ensuring that everyone understands their role at this stage is key to a successful project.

New central library for a small unitary authority

New headquarters office for high-tech internet-based company

The selected procurement route is two-stage design and build, with the contractor appointed at the end of Stage 3.

The client's architect has been retained by the local authority to monitor the design development undertaken by the contractor. They must ensure the budget submitted by the contractor at Stage 2 of the D+B negotiations is reasonable and that all of the project risks have been identified. They will have evaluated the Construction Strategy prepared by the contractor's team, ensuring that appropriate testing and samples are in place and that the new design team understand the project outcomes required.

The contractor's architect reviews and agrees the Design Responsibility Matrix with the contractor, specialist subcontractors and the design team. They develop the Design Programme and complete the fully integrated Technical Design information sufficient for construction purposes.

The design team have already obtained Building Control approval when the contractor decides to change the type of insulation in the roof. The design team prepare a change-control application, and once approved by the contractor re-examine their details and calculations and prepare an amendment to the approved Building Control application. They also confirm that the completed Technical Design satisfies the employer's requirements.

The design team have been told to assume a management contract with a construction manager and around 15 different packages of work. The architect is on a direct appointment with the client, but is not engaged to administer the project.

The design team must agree with the construction manager, the cost consultant and the client the budget for each individual package, together with the programme for production of information. Because the client is keen to progress the project, a degree of progressive fixity is introduced. This enables the contractor to start building the foundations and superstructure before the interior design is complete. It results in an overlap between Stage 4 and Stage 5.

The lead designer develops a Design Programme that indicates the critical path for progressive fixity. The Technical Design is completed, ensuring that the tender packages identify all of the interfaces between packages and that all work will be covered by the completion of the final package. The Design Responsibility Matrix is used to highlight who owns the interface between each package.

CHAPTER 04

STAGE 5
CONSTRUCTION

RIBA
Plan of
Work
2013

Stage 5

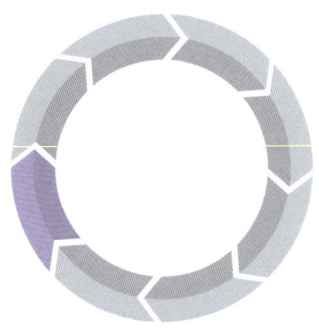

Construction

Task Bar	Tasks
Core Objectives	Offsite manufacturing and onsite **Construction** in accordance with the **Construction Programme** and resolution of **Design Queries** from site as they arise.
Procurement Variable task bar	Administration of **Building Contract**, including regular site inspections and review of progress.
Programme Variable task bar	*The RIBA Plan of Work 2013 enables this stage to overlap with a number of other stages depending on the selected procurement route.*
(Town) Planning Variable task bar	*There are no specific activities in the RIBA Plan of Work 2013, however the contractor will need to comply with any construction-specific planning conditions, such as monitoring of noise levels.*
Suggested Key Support Tasks	Review and update **Sustainability Strategy** and implement **Handover Strategy**, including agreement of information required for commissioning, training, handover, asset management, future monitoring and maintenance and ongoing compilation of **'As-constructed' Information**. Update **Construction** and **Health and Safety Strategies**. *Support tasks are now focused on health and safety on site and ensuring that the project handover and post-occupancy activities, determined earlier, are properly facilitated.*
Sustainability Checkpoints	• *Has the design stage sustainability assessment been certified?* • *Have sustainability procedures been developed with the contractor and included in the* **Construction Strategy**? • *Has the detailed commissioning and* **Handover Strategy** *programme been reviewed?* • *Confirm that the contractor's interim testing and monitoring of construction has been reviewed and observed, particularly in relation to airtightness and continuity of insulation.* • *Is the non-technical user guide complete and the aftercare service set up?* • *Has the* **'As-constructed' Information** *been issued for post-construction sustainability certification?*
Information Exchanges (at stage completion)	**'As-constructed' Information**.
UK Government Information Exchanges	Not required.

OVERVIEW

Having completed Technical Design at Stage 4, it is now time to commence the construction of the building. The responsibility for the project starts to pass to the contractor towards the end of Stage 4, and by the time they commence Stage 5 Construction the contractor must ensure that they have all of the requisite information to complete the building in accordance with the Construction Programme. The rest of the design team now take on the role of inspecting the works and ensuring that any design queries are answered. In addition to the activities to be completed on site, Stage 5 will include all of the off-site manufacture of components that have been designed for the building. This chapter will describe how to prepare for this stage. It will explain how to deal with contractor mobilisation, and what to do if you are appointed as contract administrator. It will give an insight into the approach and processes required through the construction phase of the project, and a description on how to approach the 'As-constructed' Information. It will touch briefly on the preparation required to complete the building, and how to prepare for handover and occupation.

WHAT IS STAGE 5?

During this stage, the building is constructed on site in accordance with the Technical Design information and the Construction Programme.

At the commencement of Stage 5 there is a contractor mobilisation period to enable the contractor to prepare for the construction works ahead. There is a pre-start meeting, at which the contract administrator or employer's agent leads the project team through the proposed building project, the protocols and procedures to be adopted, and the challenges ahead.

Throughout Stage 5 the design team will answer specific design queries generated by the site works, inspections of the work will be undertaken to validate quality, and progress will be monitored against the contractor's Construction Programme. As the project approaches completion, the Handover Strategy will be implemented.

At the conclusion of Stage 5, the project team will have:

- Completed the construction of the project.
- Tested and commissioned the active systems within the building.
- Completed a User Guide.
- Completed the 'As-constructed' Information.
- Put in place all appropriate certificates and approvals.

WHAT IS REQUIRED AT THE COMMENCEMENT
of Stage 5?

At the start of Stage 5 it is important to ensure that all documents are in place before construction work commences. They include the following:

- The Building Contract: Depending on the procurement route selected, this may already be in place. For design and build or management contracting, it will be completed during Stages 2 or 3. If traditional, it will need to be signed at this point by the client (employer) and the contractor. It is customary to send the contract documents first to the contractor and then to the employer for signing. Any agreed alterations should be initialled by both parties.
- Technical Design documentation: A clean set of Technical Design drawings and models should be issued to the contractor at the start of the stage. It is crucial that these are identical to the drawings that were used to agree the tender price; however, they should all be marked 'Construction' status and all revisions removed. Other documents may include a fully completed bill of quantities, specifications and schedules of work.
- Construction Programme and method statements: These will be used to monitor progress of the works, so they should be in sufficient detail to show all construction activities, the interdependence of different trades and the critical path through the programme.
- A Request for Further Information (RFI) schedule: Ideally, all information necessary for construction will be completed before Stage 5 begins. Where there are design queries about that information, an RFI schedule should be agreed in order to ensure that there is no delay to the construction.
- Administration forms: These are pre-published forms to be completed by the contract administrator, and will vary depending on the type of contract used.

WHAT ROLES ARE REQUIRED AT STAGE 5?

There are a number of important roles to fill during Stage 5 Construction:

Client and/or client adviser

The client enters into the building contract as the employer. Their role is to give the contractor possession of the site, appoint a contract administrator or an employer's agent (design and build) and pay all amounts properly certified.

Construction lead/Principal Contractor

The contractor takes on this role. They must update and implement the Construction Strategy and take ownership of the Health and Safety Strategy, in addition to understanding the project objectives and other strategy documents associated with the project. In addition, the principal contractor is responsible for producing the Construction Phase Plan and ensuring the workers have the right skills and training for the job in hand.

Project lead

They will manage the implementation of the Handover Strategy, monitor and review the performance of the project team, comment on the Construction Programme, and implement and update the Project Execution Plan.

Architect

They will carry out site inspections, review the works against specification and Construction Programme, respond to design queries as they arise and prepare the 'As-constructed' Information.

Building services engineer

They will carry out site inspections, review the works against specification and Construction Programme, respond to design queries as they arise and prepare the 'As-constructed' Information.

Civil and structural engineers

They will carry out site inspections, review the works against specification and Construction Programme, respond to design queries as they arise and prepare the 'As-constructed' Information.

Lead designer

They will carry out site inspections, review the works against specification and Construction Programme and assist design team members with responses to design queries as they arise.

Principal Designer

The principal designer retains a responsibility for considering Health and Safety issues as long as there is any design work still to complete, including identifying and eliminating risk.

Cost consultant

They will prepare valuations in accordance with the Building Contract.

Health and safety advisor

This is a useful role throughout the project. At this stage, they can assist the Principal Contractor with any update to the Health and Safety Plan and in the review of the 'As constructed information'.

Contract administrator

They will administer the Building Contract, manage the Change Control Procedures and coordinate site inspections.

It is possible for one person to take on more than one role. The scale and complexity of a project will determine whether this is possible.

UNDERTAKING MULTIPLE ROLES AS THE ARCHITECT

For example, in dealing with Scenario A, a small house extension, it would not be unusual for the architect to take on the roles of project lead, lead designer and contract administrator in addition to his or her duties as an architect. Similarly, in Scenario C, the refurbishment of a teaching facility, the architect might undertake the roles of lead designer and architect, whilst the role of contract administrator could be undertaken by a management company.

What is the role of the contract administrator at the start of Stage 5?

The contract administrator is appointed by the client to administer the contract on their behalf. Depending on the type of client organisation, this may be a fairly autonomous role or may involve the need to work very closely with the client.

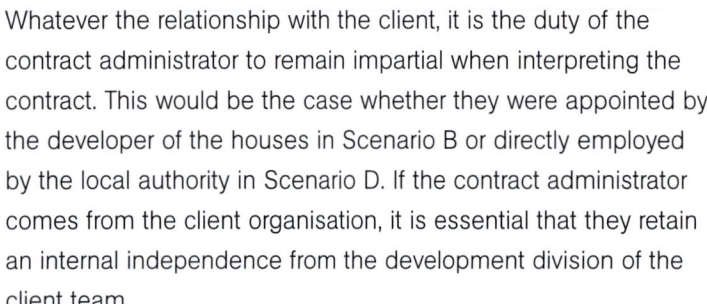

REMAINING IMPARTIAL AS THE CONTRACT ADMINISTRATOR

Whatever the relationship with the client, it is the duty of the contract administrator to remain impartial when interpreting the contract. This would be the case whether they were appointed by the developer of the houses in Scenario B or directly employed by the local authority in Scenario D. If the contract administrator comes from the client organisation, it is essential that they retain an internal independence from the development division of the client team.

The contract administrator's roles and responsibilities include the following:

- Understanding the full range of contractual requirements of the project.
- Holding regular site progress meetings, including a pre-start meeting.
- Preparing regular reports for the client on the time, quality and cost implications of the project.
- Ensuring that the contract documents are all signed and in place, including insurances.
- If in accordance with the contract conditions, dealing with claims from the contractor for either extensions of time or loss and expense.
- Issuing the appropriate certificates throughout the stage.
- Overseeing the handover procedures.

Whatever the relationship, it is important that the contract administrator instils confidence in the project team. The first real opportunity to demonstrate this comes with the pre-contract meeting. It is essential at this meeting that the contract administrator is familiar with all the contract particulars and is fully aware of any potentially difficult areas.
The contract administrator chairs this meeting, and must ensure that everyone gets the opportunity to contribute before the project starts.

At the pre-contract meeting, the contract administrator will be expected to cover the following items:

- Introduce the representatives who will regularly attend progress meetings and clarifying their roles and responsibilities. The client, contractor and design team may wish to introduce themselves.
- Briefly describe the project and its priorities, objectives and any separate contract which may be relevant (eg preliminary, client's own contractors).
- Indicate any specialists appointed by the client for this contract.
- Describe the present position with regard to preparation and signature of the contract documents.
- Hand over any outstanding Technical Design and variation instructions.
- Review the necessity for issuing other important information.
- Request that insurance documents be available for inspection immediately; reminding the contractor to check specialist subcontractors' indemnities.
- Check whether further instructions are needed for special cover.
- Confirm the existence, status and use of the information release schedule, if used. Establish the procedure for agreeing adjustments to the schedule, should they be necessary.
- Confirm the contractor's status and role as competent constructor under the CDM Regulations.

Contractor's matters

- Check that the contractor's master programme is in the format required and that it satisfactorily accommodates the specialist subcontractors. It must:
  - ~ Contain adequate separate work elements to measure their progress and integration with services installations.
  - ~ Allocate specific dates for specialist subcontract works – including supply of information, site operations, testing and commissioning.
  - ~ Accommodate public utilities, etc.
- Review in detail the particular provisions in the Building Contract concerning site access, organisation, facilities, restrictions, services, etc. to ensure that no queries remain outstanding.
- Reminding the contractor of the contractual duties to supervise, of your duties to inspect and of the site inspectorate's duties in connection with the works. Clarifying which standards, quality of work and management are required during the execution of the works. Remember: quality control is the contractor's responsibility.
- Emphasise that drawings, data, etc. received from the contractor or specialist subcontractors will be inspected (not approved) by the architect/design team, and will remain the responsibility of the originator.

- Remind the contractor that they must provide for competent testing and commissioning of services as set out in the Building Contract and that the time allocated for commissioning is not a contingency period for the main contract works.
- Remind the contractor to obtain written consent before subletting any work.

Site inspectorate matters

- Clarify that designers' inspections comprise periodic visits to meet the contractor's supervisory staff, plus spot visits.
- Remind the contractor that the site inspectorate must be provided with adequate facilities and access – together with information about site staff, equipment and operations – for their weekly reports to the contract administrator.
- Confirm procedures for checking quality control, eg through:
  - ~ Certificates, vouchers, etc. as required.
  - ~ Sample material to be submitted.
  - ~ Samples of workmanship to be submitted prior to work commencing.
  - ~ Test procedures set out in the bills of quantities.
  - ~ Adequate protection and storage.
  - ~ Visits to suppliers'/manufacturers' works.

Design team matters

- Confirm with the contractor that all specialist subcontractor design has been completed at Stage 4.
- If there is an overlap with the Stage 5 programme, emphasising that the design team will liaise with specialist subcontractors only through the contractor.
- Ensure that any residual work will not contribute to a construction delay.

Communication and procedures

- Remind the project team that the supply and flow of information will depend upon programmes being established at the start, and will proceed smoothly if:
  - ~ There is regular monitoring of the information schedules.
  - ~ RFIs are made specifically in writing, not by telephone.
  - ~ The design team responds quickly to queries.
  - ~ Policy queries are directed to the architect.
  - ~ Discrepancies are referred to the contract administrator for resolution, not the contractor.

- On receiving instructions, checking for discrepancies with existing documents; checking that the documents being used are current.
- Remind the project team that information to or from specialist subcontractors or suppliers must go via the contractor.
- Reiterate that all information issued by the design team is to be via the appropriate forms, certificates, notifications, etc. The contractor should be encouraged to use standard formats and classifications.
- Reiterate that all forms must show the distribution intended; agreeing numbers of copies of drawings and instructions required by all recipients.
- Clarify that no instructions from the client or design team can be accepted by the contractor or any subcontractor; only empowered, written instructions by the contract administrator are valid, and all verbal instructions must be confirmed in writing. Explain the relevant procedures under the Building Contract. Reminding the contractor that they should promptly notify the contract administrator of any written confirmations outstanding.
- Remind the project team that procedures for notices, applications or claims of any kind are to be strictly in accordance with the terms of the Building Contract; all such events should be raised immediately the relevant conditions occur or become evident.

Meetings

- Issuing an agenda before all contract administrator meetings, and circulating minutes promptly. Agree with the contractor and design team that:
  - ~ Minutes are to be taken as directions for an action only where specifically stated and agreed.
  - ~ Any dissent is to be notified within seven days.
  - ~ All persons attending meetings will have authority to act.
- Agree number of copies and distribution required.

For further details on the role of the contract administrator, refer to the RIBA Job Book, Ninth Edition, 5/SM3.

What other meetings are required during Stage 5?

A number of regular meetings need to take place in order to ensure that the project is proceeding as anticipated:

Site progress meetings

These are to be held regularly and on a consistent day (eg the last Thursday of each month). This ensures that all the attendees can reserve the time in their schedules, and that the people in attendance are empowered to act. The meetings should be chaired by the contract administrator, minutes should be prepared and an action list generated from those minutes. Refer to Figure 4.1 for a typical progress meeting agenda.

Technical meetings

These are arranged and chaired by the contractor in order to discuss the construction information with their subcontractors. The design team could be invited to attend if some of their information requires clarification. It is good practice at these meetings to establish a five-day and five-week 'look ahead' programme for each subcontractor.

Client review meetings

These present an opportunity to discuss with the client how the project is progressing. They should cover in detail the cost of the works, how much of the client's budget has been committed and which contingencies have been called upon. They should also keep the client informed about issues of quality and workmanship. In some cases, the client may ask to view samples of work on site. Finally, they should keep the client informed on the programme and progress on site. Refer to Figure 4.2 for an agenda for a client review meeting.

Job No: Job Title:
Date: Location

AGENDA FOR SITE PROGRESS MEETING
STAGE 5: CONSTRUCTION

		ACTION
1.	MINUTES OF LAST MEETING	
2.	CONTRACTOR'S REPORT	
	General report	
	Subcontractors meeting report	
	Progress and programme	
	Causes of delay	
	Health and Safety matters	
	Information received since last meeting	
	Information required, design queries	
	CA instructions required	
3.	SITE INSPECTION REPORT	
	Site matters	
	Quality control monitoring	
	Lost time	
	Tests observed and verified	
4.	ENGINEER'S REPORT	
	Structural works	
	Mechanical works	
	Electrical works	
5.	COST CONSULTANT'S REPORT	
6.	COMMUNICATION AND PROCEDURES	
7.	BUILDING CONTRACT COMPLETION DATE	
	Likely delays and their effect	
	Review of factors from previous meeting	
	Factors for review at next meeting	
	Revisions to completion date	
	Revisions to programme	
8.	ANY OTHER BUSINESS	
9.	DATE OF NEXT MEETING	

4.1
A specimen agenda for
a site progress meeting.

Job No:

Date:

Job Title:

Location

AGENDA FOR REVIEW MEETING
STAGE 5: CONSTRUCTION

		ACTION
1.	MINUTES OF LAST MEETING	
2.	PROJECT PROGRESS	
	General report	
	Progress and programme	
	Quality and workmanship	
	Causes of delay	
	Health and Safety matters	
3.	FINANCIAL MATTERS	
	Contract sum as adjusted	
	Additional approvals since date of last meeting	
	Any additional adjustments, eg PC sums	
	Contingency expenditure	
4.	VARIATIONS	
	Employer variations	
	Other variations	
5.	FINAL ESTIMATE	
6.	ANY OTHER BUSINESS	
7.	DATE OF NEXT MEETING	

4.2
A specimen agenda for
a client review meeting.

WHAT ARE THE KEY TASKS REQUIRED
at Stage 5?

The role of the design team changes once the project moves into construction. They switch from producing the Technical Design information into a responsive role. They may be engaged with the administration of the project; they will almost certainly be involved with carrying out site inspection and responding to design queries. Even when the administration role is carried out by an alternative team member, they may still be asked to get involved with reviewing progress and monitoring the contractor's programme.

Reviewing and monitoring the construction programme

The contractor will review and monitor their own construction programme in order to prepare their report for the regular progress meeting. The contract administrator should review it independently for the same meeting. The Construction Programme should identify the following items:

- **Activity bars:** Each construction task should be represented on the programme by an individual bar. The complexity of the task will determine the level of detail that is represented by each of the bars, but generally they will be grouped under the trade involved.
- **Critical path:** The programme should clearly identify those activities that need to be completed before the next task can begin. These linked activities form the critical path through the programme.
- **Long-lead items:** Tender dates and manufacturing periods should be identified, particularly if certain items require a long time to manufacture.
- **Float:** Where an activity can be delayed without affecting the final outcome, the extent of the delay from the planned completion date is referred to as float.

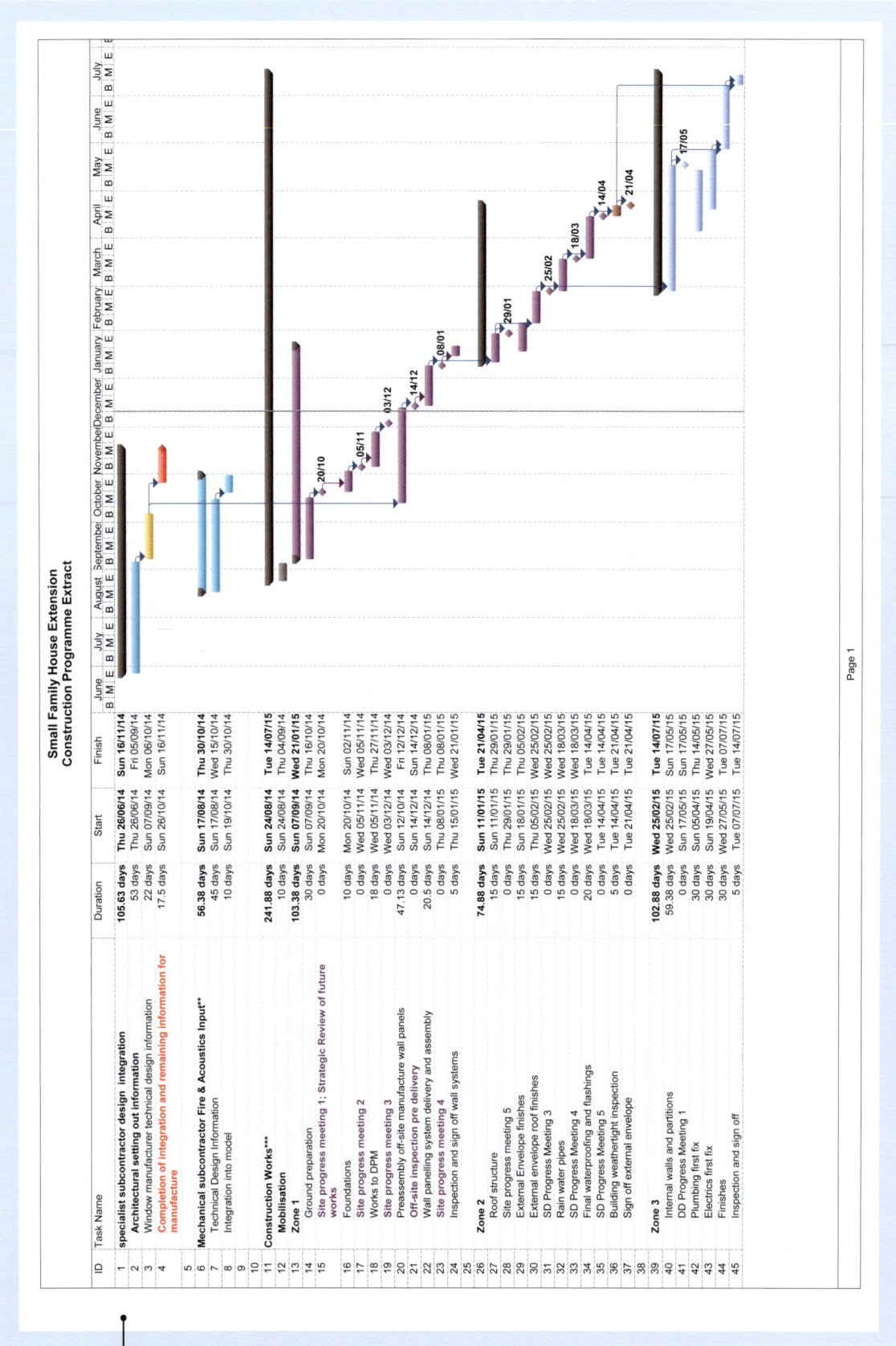

Small Family House Extension
Construction Programme Extract

ID	Task Name	Duration	Start	Finish
1	**specialist subcontractor design integration**	**105.63 days**	**Thu 26/06/14**	**Sun 16/11/14**
2	Architectural setting out information	53 days	Thu 26/06/14	Fri 05/09/14
3	Window manufacturer technical design information	22 days	Mon 06/10/14	Mon 06/10/14
4	Completion of integration and remaining information for manufacture	17.5 days	Sun 26/10/14	Sun 16/11/14
5				
6	**Mechanical subcontractor Fire & Acoustics Input****	**56.38 days**	**Sun 17/08/14**	**Thu 30/10/14**
7	Technical Design Information	45 days	Sun 17/08/14	Wed 15/10/14
8	Integration into model	10 days	Sun 19/10/14	Thu 30/10/14
9				
10				
11	**Construction Works*****	**241.88 days**	**Sun 24/08/14**	**Tue 14/07/15**
12	**Mobilisation**	**103.38 days**	**Sun 24/08/14**	**Wed 21/01/15**
13	**Zone 1**		**Sun 07/09/14**	**Wed 21/01/15**
14	Ground preparation	30 days	Sun 07/09/14	Wed 16/10/14
15	Site progress meeting 1; Strategic Review of future works	0 days	Mon 20/10/14	Mon 20/10/14
16	Foundations	10 days	Mon 20/10/14	Sun 02/11/14
17	Site progress meeting 2	0 days	Wed 05/11/14	Wed 05/11/14
18	Works to DPM	18 days	Wed 05/11/14	Thu 27/11/14
19	Site progress meeting 3	0 days	Wed 03/12/14	Wed 03/12/14
20	Preassembly off-site manufacture wall panels	47.13 days	Sun 12/10/14	Fri 12/12/14
21	Off-site inspection pre delivery	0 days	Sun 14/12/14	Sun 14/12/14
22	Wall panelling system delivery and assembly	20.5 days	Sun 14/12/14	Thu 08/01/15
23	Site progress meeting 4	0 days	Thu 08/01/15	Thu 08/01/15
24	Inspection and sign off wall systems	5 days	Thu 15/01/15	Wed 21/01/15
25				
26	**Zone 2**	**74.88 days**	**Sun 11/01/15**	**Tue 21/04/15**
27	Roof structure	15 days	Sun 11/01/15	Thu 29/01/15
28	Site progress meeting 5	0 days	Thu 29/01/15	Thu 29/01/15
29	External Envelope finishes	15 days	Sun 18/01/15	Thu 05/02/15
30	External envelope roof finishes	15 days	Thu 05/02/15	Wed 25/02/15
31	SD Progress Meeting 3	0 days	Wed 25/02/15	Wed 25/02/15
32	Rain water pipes	15 days	Wed 25/02/15	Wed 18/03/15
33	SD Progress Meeting 4	0 days	Wed 18/03/15	Wed 18/03/15
34	Final waterproofing and flashings	20 days	Wed 18/03/15	Tue 14/04/15
35	SD Progress Meeting 5	0 days	Tue 14/04/15	Tue 14/04/15
36	Building weathertight inspection	5 days	Tue 14/04/15	Tue 21/04/15
37	Sign off external envelope	0 days	Tue 21/04/15	Tue 21/04/15
38				
39	**Zone 3**	**102.88 days**	**Wed 25/02/15**	**Tue 14/07/15**
40	Internal walls and partitions	59.38 days	Wed 25/02/15	Sun 17/05/15
41	DD Progress Meeting 1	0 days	Sun 17/05/15	Sun 17/05/15
42	Plumbing first fix	30 days	Sun 05/04/15	Thu 14/05/15
43	Electrics first fix	30 days	Sun 19/04/15	Tue 14/05/15
44	Finishes	30 days	Wed 27/05/15	Tue 07/07/15
45	Inspection and sign off	5 days	Tue 07/07/15	Tue 14/07/15

Page 1

4.3

A simple extract from a contractor's programme.

When the programme is complete, the contractor's progress can be monitored at the monthly site progress meetings. In addition to the contractor's assessment of progress, the contract administrator should determine their own view. This can be done by a visual inspection of the works, an assessment of the valuation certificates against planned expenditure, and a review of the contractor's programme. At the progress meeting, the contract administrator should agree with the contractor a combined view on progress and ascertain any plans the contractor may have for ensuring that the building is delivered on time.

How to prepare for a site visit to inspect the works

The architect is generally one of the most important members of the project team when it comes to undertaking a site inspection. They will have a good working knowledge of all the architectural components and, as the project lead during design and the lead coordinator of the project, they will be familiar with how the whole of the building should be assembled. This gives them the opportunity to inspect the works that are completed as well as looking out for future issues before they become a problem.

Site visits should have a specific purpose, and as such require preparation beforehand. The first task is to review the most recent site reports and minutes of meetings. Secondly, review the drawings of the particular area that you intend to inspect. Prepare a small pack of drawing extracts and specification items that you may wish to refer to. Although spot checks, without prior notice, can be effective, consider the complexity of the work you intend to inspect. Are there particular subcontractors that you would like to talk to, or will work have to be suspended in that area while you gain access for inspection? If these or any other special circumstances prevail, it is best to give notice to the construction team before you visit.

It is important at all times to be fully aware of the health and safety issues present on the construction site. Ensure that you are equipped with the appropriate safety clothing. As a minimum this should include steel-protected boots/shoes, a safety hat, eye protection, finger protection and high-visibility jacket. Other items may be required, such as ear defenders or harnesses; if these are provided for you, then you should be satisfied that they are appropriate for the task in hand. Inform your own office that you intend to visit the site, giving the date and time. This will ensure, in the event of an accident, that someone is expecting you to return.

The contractor is responsible for ensuring that all visitors to site are inducted into the specific safety features of the site. They are obligated to make you aware of any revisions to the safe routes across the site, permit-to-work areas and any specific activities that may have an impact on your safety. It might be a requirement of the contract documents that the team carrying out site inspections have to demonstrate their safety awareness through an accredited certificate or safety qualification. If this is the case, then the project team will need to obtain this training before they can visit the site.

During the visit, ensure that everything is recorded in a consistent way. Photographs are a good way to record progress and specific concerns that you wish to raise. These should be supplemented with systematic notes. A good tip is to identify a vantage point at the start of a project that will facilitate a record of progress as the building work proceeds. It is often useful to refer back to these photographs and notes in order to assist with the evaluation of a claim from the contractor or to verify an interim certificate that describes the work as properly executed. Quite often during a visit from the project team, a query will be raised or a suggestion made by the contractor on an alternative method. Remember, all instructions to the contractor must go through the contract administrator. Be aware that any alternative is likely to lead to a claim for additional time and/or money. Because of this, change should be avoided at Stage 5. If it appears essential, then the full implications of time and cost must be understood before considering it.

The number of visits to site will have been agreed with the client in the appointment for Stage 5. If more frequent visits than envisaged – or, indeed, constant inspection – is required, then the client should be advised to appoint a resident site inspector or a clerk of works. Their contribution should not be regarded by the architect as 'supervision', as such appointees do not necessarily have the authority to issue instructions.

Figure 4.4 illustrates a typical page from a site report, and shows:

- The junction of the ceiling rafts is not in line with the bulkhead. Check the detail and discuss with the contractor. The galvanised metalwork is specified to be painted black above the ceiling. Highlight to the contractor.
- The roof liner can be seen from inside the building. Detail to be checked and highlighted to the contractor.
- Colour variations across the timber panels will need to be reviewed against any samples provided by the supplier.

Job No: Job Title:

Date: Location

SITE PROGRESS REPORT
STAGE 5: CONSTRUCTION

SITE PHOTO RECORD	COMMENT	ACTION
1.	**CEILING RAFTS** 1. Spacing of ceiling panels is inconsistent with setting out shown on drawing 2. Galvanised support above ceiling is not blacked out 3. Junction with vertical bulkhead is not as shown on drawing	Const. Lead Const. Lead Const. Lead
2.	**ROOFLIGHT** 1. Black liner applied to edge of roof light is visible from interior	Const. Lead Roof Const.
3.	**COLOUR CONSISTENCY** 1. Sprinkler valve fitted in panelling system prior to colour variation being agreed. Panels to be inspected and relocated 2. Panels to be reviewed to comply with colour sample agreed at outset.	Const. Lead Arch Arch

4.4

A typical page from a
site report.

115

Issuing certificates during Stage 5

Throughout Stage 5, a number of documents are issued by the contract administrator to the contractor. They usually require certain conditions to be satisfied. They may vary in format and content between differing Building Contracts, although they will all be statements of fact. They could include the following:

- Interim Certificate: This certifies payment to the contractor. It is important to ensure that the cost consultant's valuation is supported by confirmation from the inspection team that the work has been completed to an acceptable standard.
- Statement of retention: This is generally attached to the Interim Certificate, it should clearly state the sums to be retained until the end of the project.
- Contract administrator's instructions: These are used to inform the contractor of developments or changes in the works from the original construction documents. Under a design and build contract, they are usually referred to as employer's agent instructions.
- Sectional Completion Certificate: This is used on large projects where it has been agreed in advance that the building can be handed over in phases.
- Practical Completion Certificate: This is issued when the works have been finished and the employer can take possession of the building. It creates an obligation to release a proportion of the retention monies.
- Notification of revision to the completion date: This is issued when an extension of time has been granted or the works are not finished at the planned Practical Completion inspection.
- Non-completion Certificate: This is issued when the works are not completed on time. This certificate could trigger damages under the contract.

Two further certificates – the Certificate of Making Good and the Final Certificate – are issued at Stage 6.

Resolving Design Queries, RFI monitoring and recording

Design queries during construction occur when the information provided to the contractor is incomplete or inconsistent, or a discovery on site has resulted in earlier assumptions being challenged. Incomplete documentation may include instances in which the tender information was confined to scope information only, and the contractor now needs the detailed setting-out information. Inconsistency may involve information describing a product or component contradicting itself, requiring clarification. On projects such as the university refurbishment (Scenario C), site exploration works may expose existing conditions that had not been anticipated, and the contractor will ask for direction from the design team.

SPECIFICATION NOTES ON DRAWINGS

Avoid repeating notes on the drawing that are contained in the specification. Any updates to the specification may not make their way onto an updated drawing, which could result in contradictory information. In principle, avoid duplication of information and refer to things once only, in the correct place.

It is important to ensure that the contractor raises any queries they may have on the construction documentation in a formal way. Create a log of each Request for Information (RFI), record the date received, the date by which an answer is required and the date it was answered. This may prove useful later when determining any claim for an extension of time from the contractor. Note that the date by which an RFI must be answered is often determined by the contract and not always by the contractor's programme demands. Ensure, during the regular progress meetings, that the contractor is looking well ahead. This will lead to a reasonable time for the project team to respond to any such requests.

How to deal with a claim/extension of time

The contract administrator only has the authority to act where the Building Contract conditions expressly give them this entitlement. Most construction contracts include mechanisms for dealing with extensions of time and loss or expense applications. When dealing with such claims, the following should be borne in mind:

Extensions of time

Generally these arise when events that might affect progress are beyond the control of the contractor and were not foreseeable at the time of tender. There may be an express definition in the Building Contract of the terms that allow the contract administrator to grant an extension of time. Usually the extension results in a waiver of liquidated damages together with expenses relating to the extended period, such as retaining site welfare facilities for a longer period.

When dealing with extensions of time, the RIBA Job Book, Ninth Edition, provides the following checklist:

- Respond to each and every proper notice of delay from the contractor to demonstrate that the claim has been properly considered.
- When awarding extensions of time, do so only for the causes specified in the Building Contract. State the causes but do not apportion. Keep full records in case the award is contested.
- Comply strictly with the procedural rules.
- Observe the timescales quoted in the Building Contract.
- Form an opinion which is fair and reasonable in the light of the information available at the time.

Loss and/or expense applications

The contract administrator only has the authority to settle claims that are identified in the Building Contract. For a loss/expense application to be valid:

- The loss and/or expense must be a direct actual loss.
- The works must be materially affected.
- Interference to regular planned progress must have occurred.
- Reimbursement must not be possible under any other contract provision.

It is important to reach a fair and reasonable conclusion. The contractor must provide the contract administrator with enough information to substantiate their claim. This should be evaluated against the latter's own observations, which may have been recorded in site reports, itemisation of defective work on valuation certificates and/or in site progress meetings.

SCENARIO B: DEVELOPMENT OF FIVE NEW HOMES FOR A SMALL RESIDENTIAL DEVELOPER

The contractor is excavating the site when they discover additional underground services beneath the location of house no. 4 that were not shown on the 'As Existing' drawings. The services have to be relocated outside the curtilage of the new dwelling, and this takes an extra seven days to complete before work can continue on the affected property. The contractor writes to the contract administrator requesting an extension of time for seven days.

The contract administrator reviews the claim with the appropriate members of the design team. They consider that seven days was a reasonable time to relocate the services, and that whilst there was only a delay to house no. 4 this did affect the critical path progress on all the houses. They agree an extension of seven working days.

WHAT ARE THE KEY SUPPORT TASKS
at this stage?

Updating the Health and Safety Strategy

At the commencement of Stage 5 it is important to hold a risk workshop with the contractor in order to review all risks that have been identified on the project. The project team will have completed their design risk register prior to construction commencing. A number of risk items may have been impossible to mitigate until the contractor or their specialist subcontractors were appointed. The health and safety advisor should lead this activity, as well as ensuring that the following items are addressed:

- Informing the contract administrator that the welfare facilities provided by the contractor are adequate.
- Ensuring that temporary works are covered by an appropriate risk assessment.
- Reviewing and collating, together with the construction team, the Health and Safety File for inclusion in the Building Owner's Manual.
- Reviewing compliance with the brief, Building Regulations and contract requirements.
- Advising the client on the future use of the Health and Safety File.

Updating and implementing the Sustainability Strategy

As the project enters construction, it is important to ensure that the Sustainability Strategy underpinning the design is delivered by the construction team. There are some key items for the design team to develop with the contractor:

- The Site Waste Management Plan can now be finalised. This can contribute effectively to energy-saving targets.

- Consider the Transportation Plans for all materials. Ensure that local sourcing of materials and suppliers is used wherever practical.
- Explain, to the contractor, the key design elements that are essential to meet the sustainability targets.
- Work with the contractor to ensure that any phasing of the works avoids wasting energy and is as economical as possible.

Once construction work is under way, then the design team members commence a monitoring role. They will:

- Review and observe any testing that the contractor undertakes.
- Monitor construction – in particular, inspecting airtightness and continuity of insulation.
- Examine any proposed changes to the specification, to ensure that the alternative product still reaches the agreed sustainability criteria.
- If required, submit final information for statutory approval and certification, including for Building Regulations Part L compliance.

As construction comes to an end the focus of attention turns to the handover of the building, the creation of a non-technical User Guide and the proposed aftercare service required. The focus is on ensuring that the future users know how to operate the building.

WHAT IS TO BE INCLUDED

in the Information Exchanges?

The key documents that form the bulk of the Stage 5 Information Exchange must be complete in order that the client can take the project over from the contractor. A guide to the contents of these documents is as follows:

The Building Contract

This will have been duly signed and initialled, as appropriate, by the contractor and the employer.

The Health and Safety File

This will have been commenced during Stage 5 and completed by the contractor as they prepare for handover. It needs to be signed off by the health and safety advisor, and should contain:

- A description of the project, including safe working loads and structural principles.
- The residual risk register, highlighting any areas of concern that the client should be aware of and any hazards that remain.
- Manufacturers' data on equipment and components fitted in the building, particularly related to operation and maintenance.
- Details of any maintenance regimes that will be required.
- Proposals for cleaning the building, inside and out.
- The location and nature of significant services, particularly if they are concealed.

The 'As-constructed' Information

Before Stage 5 is commenced, the design team should agree with the employer and the contractor who is responsible for producing the 'As-constructed' Information and the extent of the detail required. For many employers this may be restricted to general-arrangement drawings showing the plans, sections and elevations of the building. The scale should be sufficient to define the scope of the building and its components, typically 1:100 or 1:50. In some instances, typical or important details may be included; these should give an indication of the construction methods used across the project.

In addition to drawn information, specifications should be included – as should any schedules of fixtures and fittings. It may also be appropriate to include the current trade literature for specified products as well as their recommended maintenance regimes.

Much of this information may be transferred to the client maintenance team as a Building Information Model (BIM). This could contain a digital database highlighting product information and maintenance regimes, which could assist the client team in running the building efficiently.

The User Guide to the building

Just like a car manual, the User Guide should constitute a step-by-step instruction manual for the new owner, illustrating how the building is designed to work. It should contain:

- The principles behind the design of the building, and how these affect its operation.
- The building's standards of performance.
- Any energy-saving measures.
- Water-saving measures.
- Means of operating heating, lighting and cooling systems, and the impact of incorrect operation.
- Access, security and safety systems.
- Methodology for dealing with any problems.
- Waste-management proposals.
- Car parking and cycling provision, local public transport provision.
- Training and staff induction plans.
- It may also include guidance for facilities managers, and for maintenance and other contractors.

SUMMARY

Throughout this chapter we have recognised the different roles that are required as the project moves through Stage 5 Construction, and how those roles are distinct even though they may be undertaken by the same individual on a relatively small project. We have looked in detail at the role of the contract administrator and given practical advice to those members of the design team who will need to visit site, monitor progress and inspect the works. There is a section dealing with RFIs, design queries and contractor claims for an extension of time and/or loss and expense. In the next chapter, we will examine what happens as the contractor hands over the project at the end of Stage 5 and the construction contract is closed out.

A Small residential extension for a growing family

B Development of five new homes for a small residential developer

SCENARIO SUMMARIES

WHAT HAS HAPPENED TO OUR PROJECTS BY THE END OF STAGE 5?

The architect in his role as contract administrator has determined that an extension of time is due to the contractor because of changes to the ground-floor layout requested by the client. As the new completion date is approaching, a pre-handover meeting is held with the contractor and the client is invited to attend. There is an opportunity to inspect the construction works to make sure that the final quality standards have been met. Both the client and the architect are delighted with the quality of the works.

The new heating system is commissioned and tested, but fails to operate successfully. It looks like the project will be delayed as a new part is ordered. The contract administrator decides to delay handover until this element of the work is functioning properly. The retention money is held back from the contractor, but no further damages are applied as the family, who are living in the existing house, are not financially penalised by the delay.

The houses approach Practical Completion, but a final inspection of the works reveals numerous small defects in each of the buildings mainly related to the internal walls. The developer is keen to take ownership of the properties, as he has promised them to the new owners. The architect makes a comprehensive list of rectification works and agrees these with the contractor. Each of the owners are contacted by the developer to explain that the access to the properties will be required by the contractor to rectify the defects and a programme of work is agreed. The programme and the rectification schedule are attached to the Practical Completion Certificate. The retention monies are partly released, but those relating to the defective work are retained.

The design team prepare a User Guide for the developer, and the contractor completes the Health and Safety File.

Refurbishment of a teaching and support building for a university

The novated design team respond to requests from the contractor for them to visit site throughout construction, to ensure that the building is completed in accordance with the construction documentation. As the project approaches completion, the novated design team also assist the contractor in preparing the Health and Safety File and the User Guide to the building. They prepare the 'As-constructed' drawings from information supplied by the contractor, and undertake a final inspection of the works, on behalf of the contractor, to validate that all the work reaches the standard specified.

New central library for a small unitary authority

The client's design team attend all progress meetings on behalf of the client, to ensure that the works are proceeding in accordance with the contractor's Construction Programme. They regularly inspect the works to ensure that they comply with the contract information. Once a month, the cost consultant and the client's design team agree a valuation for the works before reporting this to the client's project board.

The contractor's design team ensure that all design queries are answered as they arise. They assist the contractor in the preparation and update of the BIM information for handing over to the client at the end of the project. A number of maintenance dates are attached to the equipment icons contained in the BIM information, to assist the client in the operation and maintenance of the building. Practical completion is granted and the building is handed over one week early.

New headquarters office for high-tech internet-based company

The individual packages reach completion at different times, as the project is sequentially completed. The design team and the management contractor agree to sign off each package after making a detailed inspection and a full photographic record of each handover is made. (The photographic record is important to ensure that no arguments arise if another package contractor damages the work after it has been handed over.)

As the project approaches practical completion, the design team undertake a full inspection of the works with the contractor to produce an agreed rectification list.

The managing contractor puts together an overall Health and Safety File for the client.

CHAPTER 05

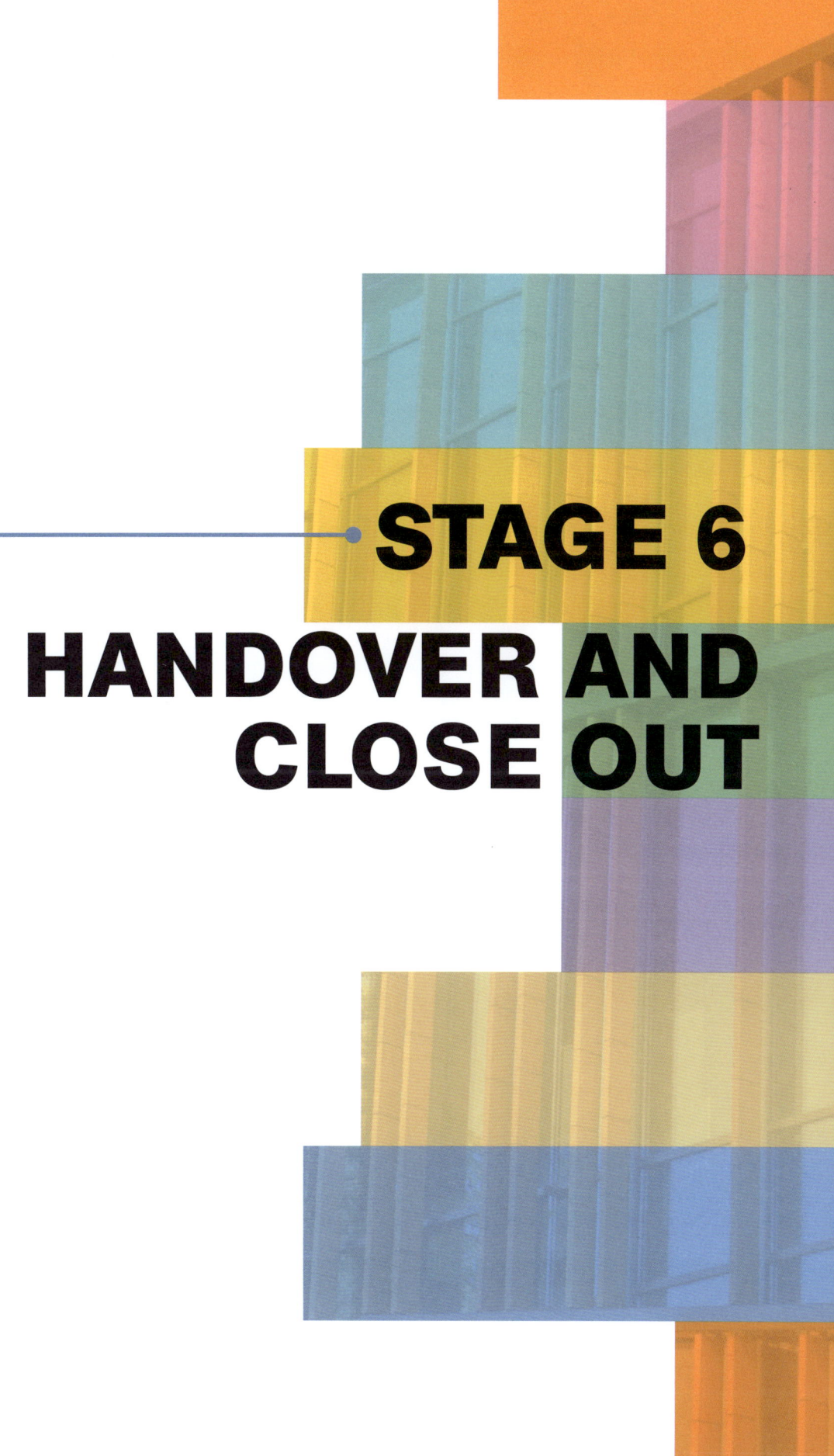

STAGE 6

HANDOVER AND CLOSE OUT

RIBA
Plan of
Work
2013

Stage 6

Handover
and Close Out

Task Bar	Tasks
Core Objectives	Handover of building and conclusion of **Building Contract**.
Procurement *Variable task bar*	Conclude administration of **Building Contract**.
Programme *Variable task bar*	*There are no specific activities in the RIBA Plan of Work 2013.*
(Town) Planning *Variable task bar*	*There are no specific activities in the RIBA Plan of Work 2013.*
Suggested Key Support Tasks	Carry out activities listed in **Handover Strategy** including **Feedback** for use during the future life of the building or on future projects. Updating of **Project Information** as required. *The priority during this stage is the successful handover of the building and concluding the **Building Contract** with support tasks focused on evaluating performance and providing **Feedback** for use on future projects. Fine tuning of the building services is likely to occur.*
Sustainability Checkpoints	• *Has assistance with the collation of post-completion information for final sustainability certification been provided?*
Information Exchanges (at stage completion)	Updated **'As-constructed' Information**.
UK Government Information Exchanges	Required.

OVERVIEW

Planning for Stage 6 Handover and Close Out started during Stage 1 Preparation and Brief. It was at that stage that the Project Objectives and Quality Objectives were first considered. The Sustainability Aspirations were also developed at Stage 1. These were all influential in the formation of the Handover Strategy, also commenced at Stage 1. As the project progressed through the various stages, the Handover Strategy was reviewed and updated as more detailed information came to light. Now it is time to implement that Handover Strategy. This chapter will describe the activities to be completed leading up to handover. It will highlight the responsibilities of different members of the project team at this stage. What happens at handover will be covered, and there will be a description of the post-occupancy evaluation services that may be commissioned by the client to monitor the building during Stage 7 In Use.

Unlike with the other stages, the commencement of Stage 6 Handover and Close Out is not predicated on the completion of Stage 5 Construction. Stage 6 must be started some time before Practical Completion is reached in order that the services installation can be adequately commissioned, the project team have sufficient time to ensure that the appropriate quality is reached, and the documentation can be prepared for the completion of the project. This chapter will describe what happens immediately prior to handover and at handover itself, what documentation to archive, how to induct the client owner of the building into the way in which it is designed and works, and how to obtain feedback on the building in use.

WHAT IS STAGE 6?

The core objective of Stage 6 is to achieve a successful handover of the building to the client and close out the construction contract. This stage therefore covers the activities leading from the commissioning of the building systems right up to the issue of the Final Certificate at the end of the rectification period, generally 12 months after Practical Completion. The scope for this stage can be wide-ranging, and should be agreed with the client at the outset of the project. Should the 'Soft Landings' framework be adopted for the Handover Strategy, then this process needs to start at Stage 1. Even when it isn't adopted there is the potential to introduce a wide-ranging scope of services, which may include:

- Attending feedback workshops.
- Considering how lessons learnt can be adopted for the benefit of the project team.
- Undertaking an initial Post-Occupancy Evaluation that considers whether the desired Project Outcomes have been achieved.
- Undertaking tasks related to the successful operation and management of the building.

IMPLEMENTING THE HANDOVER STRATEGY

To ensure a successful project, the Handover Strategy will be prepared at Stage 1 and continually reviewed and updated as the project progresses. As the building approaches the end of construction, the project team focus on the preparations required to successfully hand over the project to the client. The range of activities should include the following:

- Commissioning, testing and witnessing the services installation.
- Inspecting the construction works for quality compliance.
- Completing the Health and Safety File.
- Developing the User Guide to the building.
- Preparing for the handover meeting.
- Starting to consider feedback workshops on the building and the process of design and construction.
- Establishing the method and responsibilities for Post-Occupancy Evaluation.
- Adopting the 'Soft Landings' approach to building handover.

Commissioning, testing and witnessing the services installation

Commissioning the services installation for a building can take between three and six months depending on the complexity of the installation. It is a process that must be carefully considered to ensure that the equipment is satisfactory for its intended use. In some instances it will be necessary to undertake a number of tests – for instance, an initial test to ensure that the individual piece of equipment is satisfactory and then a further test once the whole installation is complete. This latter test may take the form of an operational readiness period, during which the services are run in their final installed state in order to demonstrate compliance. In any event, for commissioning to be successful it needs to follow a consistent process. The list below gives a general guide to a successful outcome when commissioning specific equipment.

1. Check the documentation: Make sure that all the relevant manuals and instructions are available. Check that everything that is mentioned in the documentation is available and functioning on the equipment.
2. Prepare the equipment for use: Carry out any relevant 'warm-up' processes. Allow the equipment to go through any built-in self-check or -test programmes on start-up.
3. Undertake safety tests: Ensure that all electrical equipment is tested for adequate insulation and earth connections. Consider mechanical-safety aspects, visually inspect the equipment and study drawings.
4. Initial calibration: Adjust the equipment to prevailing conditions, climate, electricity supply and altitude, so that the readings are true.
5. Calibration: Ensure that the equipment is set to provide dependable and accurate results – for instance, set room thermostats to achieve appropriate temperatures.
6. Function tests: Run the manufacturers' recommended methods and protocols, ensuring that the results are acceptable. If possible, process a few control samples of known value to make sure that the equipment is functioning properly.
7. Record the results: Keep records of all results in the Health and Safety File. Complete an acceptance log sheet when the work has been completed satisfactorily and all tests have been passed.

Inspecting the construction work for quality compliance

As the building approaches handover, the contractor will offer up areas of work for final inspection. If the quality of building work has been regularly examined throughout construction, then this is likely to hold few surprises. None the less, it is important that this final inspection is carried out in a systematic way, as Practical Completion can only be achieved when the building is reasonably free from defects.

First impressions are useful in establishing if the building is ready for its final inspection. Take a moment to consider if all the building work has been completed. If there are any omissions, then defer the inspection. Do not be persuaded to inspect incomplete work; it will only have to be done again when finished. Check that all the fittings in each room have been provided and are working properly. Compare the accommodation to your room data sheets prepared during Stages 2–4. Consider the temperature of the room, and whether it is presented at an appropriate temperature. Once you have established that the space is ready for inspection, commence in a structured way, starting in one corner and working your way around the room. Open all the windows, examine the finishes for blemishes and marks; remember, at this stage the building should be presented in pristine condition.

The design team should complete their final inspection and then discuss any areas of concern with the contractor. Ideally the rectification of any defects should be completed before handover, but this is not always possible – particularly if the defective part is a manufactured component with a fabrication lead-in time. If this is the case, the design team will need to decide if the building can function effectively with the defect in place after Practical Completion. If not, then a non-completion notice will need to be completed by the contract administrator and a close-out programme agreed with the contractor. If, in the opinion of the contract administrator, the building can adequately be occupied, the defect is appended to the Practical Completion Certificate. In this instance, it is critical to agree the programme for the rectification of defects with the contractor prior to signing the Practical Completion Certificate. It will also be necessary to agree entry times and levels of disruption to be anticipated by the client/users of the building.

DELIVERING A HIGH-QUALITY PRODUCT

The project team can increase the probability of a high-quality product by adopting some simple mitigation measures throughout construction:

- Incorporate mock-ups of important features, so that these can be evaluated well in advance of critical construction dates.
- Agree a separate sample of the work with the contractor before work commences. Ensure it is in an area of the site where it can be referred to until the end of the project.
- Immediately work commences on the main project, establish a routine of regular and systematic inspections.
- As individual packages commence, designate an appropriate area as an in situ quality sample.
- Discuss any concerns with the contractor as soon as they arise.

What is on the agenda at the pre-handover meeting?

Prior to the actual handover, it is best practice to hold a pre-handover meeting to ensure that all will go smoothly at the handover. This meeting is best held two weeks prior to handover, and the following areas should be covered:

- Health and Safety Manual: This should have been handed over to the health and safety advisor two weeks before completion. The meeting is an opportunity to discuss with the contractor any missing information.
- Maintenance manuals: Again, if these are prepared early for the design team and client to review, this is an opportunity to discuss any gaps in the information.
- 'As-constructed' Information: Review status and agree final content.
- Close-out timings and protocols: Agree with the contractor when areas will be available for inspection, who will be in attendance and what tests will be carried out in the last two weeks.
- Areas where work is unsatisfactory: Highlight any concerns that may impact on the handover of the building in order to give the contractor the opportunity to address them before handover day.
- Contractual matters: Review outstanding variation orders and instructions. Ensure that valuations are up to date, and everything is in place to prepare the handover account.
- Site issues: Discuss the removal of site accommodation; welfare facilities; site security, if the hoarding is to come down; services connections; and any temporary services required.
- Client issues: Agree with the client their intentions post-handover, particularly if there is going to be a follow-on fit-out contract. Ensure that the contractor understands the next steps, so that the building is handed over in a suitable condition.

PRACTICAL COMPLETION
What happens at handover?

Issuing the Practical Completion Certificate

Once all the works described in the contract have been carried out, the contract administrator issues the Practical Completion Certificate. Depending on the type of contract, this has the effect of:

- Ending the contractor's liability for liquidated damages.
- Releasing half of the money that was retained from the contractor at each evaluation – usually 1.5% of the value of the works, with the remaining 1.5% reserved until final certification in 12 months' time.
- Signifying the commencement of the rectification period. This is not a period during which the contractor can finish the works or correct problems apparent at Practical Completion. It is a period in which the contractor could be called back to rectify any defects that appear once the building is occupied.
- Releasing the contractor from any performance bond taken out on the project.
- If a construction management contract, then a separate Practical Completion Certificate could be required for each package of work. This can complicate the rectification period as some of the work, whilst being practically complete, may not be able to be used until the building is complete. This latter date is when the 12-month rectification period should run from, and this should be agreed with the package contractors at tender stage.

What happens at the formal handover meeting?

The formal handover meeting is to be attended by the contract administrator, the client (or their representative), the people who will be responsible for the maintenance of the building, the design team and the contractor. Depending on the scale of the project, it is wise to allow a whole day for the proceedings.

The meeting is generally preceded by a walk around the site in order to confirm that everything is clean and tidy. A suggested format for the meeting is as follows:

- The design team should confirm that the building is ready for occupation by the client. If there are any outstanding items, they should confirm that these are of a minor nature, and that there is an agreed list of them with the contractor and an agreed programme for completion. If these items are many, or of significance, then the handover will have to be deferred.
- The contractor confirms that Building Control inspectors have made their final inspection, and a completion certificate has been issued.
- The contractor confirms that all statutory inspections and approvals have been satisfactorily completed.
- The contractor confirms that all tests have been satisfactorily completed, witnessed and certified.
- The design team undertake a final inspection of the key building documents, handed over by the contractor, to enable the client to run the building. These will include:
  - ~ The Health and Safety File: This must contain information about the structure and materials in the building – and in particular, any effect that they may have on anyone cleaning, maintaining, altering or demolishing part or all of the building.
  - ~ The Operation and Maintenance Manuals: These should contain As-Constructed drawings, recording construction and indicating the routes of all services installed. Copies of manufacturers' current literature should be included for all products, including recommendations for cleaning and maintenance. A directory of all subcontractors, suppliers and manufacturers should be included, along with copies of test certificates and reports, guarantees, warranties and any maintenance agreements.
  - ~ A User Guide to the building: The client is to confirm that they understand how the building is intended to operate, and that their maintenance team have received appropriate training.
- Agreement is reached on methods of future access to the site and procedures to be followed after Practical Completion.
- Procedures are also established for agreeing the end of the rectification period and issuing the Final Certificate.

THE IMPACT OF BIM ON HANDOVER DOCUMENTATION

The introduction of BIM will change the documentation that the contractor includes in their Information Exchange at handover. The project information will be capable of containing digital data on the maintenance regime for the systems in the building, all the health and safety information and the 'As-constructed' digital information, together with any links to trade literature. The model could be handed to the client to assist them in operating the building, allowing them to control their environment through the digital information. For this to be successful, the design team will need to be working towards this goal from the outset of the design.

Following satisfactory completion of the handover meeting, a Practical Completion Certificate can be issued. At this stage, there are a number of other matters to conclude:

- The keys to the building are to be handed to the client.
- Meter readings are to be taken of all utilities.
- The client takes over responsibility for insuring the building.
- The final account is settled with the contractor.

It is also wise to complete a full photographic record of the completed building, together with any marketing or publicity images that may be beneficial.

Providing a collateral warranty

The contract administrator should make sure that all the appointment documents are completed before the building is signed off. The contract for both the contractor and the design team will have been completed at the start of their commissions. If within those documents collateral warranties were requested, then they could be actioned following Practical Completion. A warranty conveys to other interested parties, who are not in direct contract, some or all of the contractual rights existing between the client employer and the contractor or consultant. This category may include a future owner of the building, an institutional investor or an occupant of the building. There is no obligation to provide warranties that were not requested in the original contract documents.

Using 'Soft Landings' to ensure a smooth handover from construction to occupation

The transition from construction to occupation can be a difficult period. The contractor will be focusing on completing construction in order to avoid any penalties associated with a delay. The design team will generally be concerned with establishing that everything is built correctly, and they will be producing the 'As-constructed' Information. The client will generally be enthusiastic to take possession of the building and commence occupation. In order to assist with a smooth transition a framework for the approach to handing over a building to a client has been developed by the Building Services Research and Information Association (BSRIA) and the Usable Buildings Trust. This framework is called Soft Landings, and it covers five key points that need to be addressed at various stages of the RIBA Plan of Work 2013:

- **Stage 1:** Ensure that the clients' needs and required outcomes are clearly defined.
- **Stages 2 and 3:** Review comparable projects and assess proposals in relation to facilities management and building users.
- **Stage 5**: Ensure that the maintenance team and operators know how the building works before occupation. Compile the Building User Guide.
- **Stage 6:** Station a team on site to receive feedback as the building comes into use. Fine-tune the systems and ensure optimum operation.
- **Stage 7:** Extended aftercare allows any outstanding issue to be resolved and feedback obtained for future projects.

The key activity at Stage 6 Handover and Close Out is to help the client achieve optimum performance from the building. It may involve design team members being on site for a number of weeks before and after Practical Completion. It may also involve using the Building Information Model to assist in calibrating the services operating in the building. This is an additional duty for members of the design team, and this aspect of a Handover Strategy should be raised with the client at the outset when fees are being agreed at Stage 1.

Completing an energy assessment on completion of the building

It is best practice for all buildings to have an Energy Performance Certificate (EPC) on completion; for some buildings, such as new residential projects, it is mandatory. The minimum information that should be provided on the certificate includes:

- The asset rating of the building.
- A reference value or benchmark.
- A recommendation for improvements, unless there is no reasonable potential for these.
- The reference number and address of the building.
- The total usable floor area.
- The date it was issued; EPCs generally last 10 years.

A further final energy assessment may be required if other performance standards such as BREEAM (Building Research Establishment Environmental Assessment Method) or LEED (Leadership in Energy and Environmental Design) were used during design, in order to establish the building's performance. BREEAM addresses the sustainability issues that arise in new construction by examining the following nine categories: management, health and wellbeing, energy, transport, water, materials, waste, land use and ecology, and pollution. Within these categories, issues such as acoustic performance and the responsible sourcing of materials are considered. At the end of the project it is possible to replace the assumed design assessment with the real conditions, and create a robust post-occupancy evaluation score for the building.

FURTHER READING ON ENERGY ASSESSMENTS

For more information, refer to the Guide to BREEAM published by RIBA Publishing.

WHAT ARE THE OUTSTANDING TASKS
now that the building is ready for occupation?

Now that the building is 'practically complete' and a certificate has been issued to that effect, the client will want to move in. For many buildings, this will not occur on the day after handover. In complex buildings, there is likely to be a separate fit-out contract for the client and/or an operational readiness period. The latter is when the building systems are run at capacity before full occupation has taken place. Those first few weeks of operating the new building are a great source of information to feed into future projects. The design team should promote their appointment for additional post-occupancy evaluation services in order to benefit from this information.

What kind of feedback should be obtained?

The most useful feedback is that which covers qualitative, commercial and technical responses to the building. The following list gives a guide to the topics that should be considered.

Qualitative:
- How well does the building meet the perceived needs?
- What is the overall level of comfort?
- How satisfied is the user with the performance of the building?
- Has the building improved methods of working?
- Has the building encouraged unexpected or additional uses?

Commercial:
- Was the building delivered within the budget?
- Do you think the building represents good value for money?
- Was the building delivered on time?
- Does the building's running cost match the anticipated budget? This is not always easy to evaluate in the first few months, and more accurate results may be obtained after 12 months.
- Does the building encourage more efficient ways of working?

Technical:

- What is the typical temperature in various locations in the building? Does it meet the design temperature benchmark?
- What are the lighting levels in the different environments, day and night?
- What is the air quality like?
- How thorough is the airtightness?
- How much fuel is the building using? An early indication may suggest adjustments that could be made.

It is a common mistake to believe that buildings are operationally complete because they are 'practically complete'. Modern buildings need to work in compatible ways with their environment. A series of regular workshops shortly following the building occupation, with reviews of energy consumption and qualitative performance measures as the agenda, will give the design team an opportunity to ensure that the building is working as designed and to gain feedback for their next project.

Closing down the project in the office

Once the building is completed and before the design team is disbanded, it is good practice to document the project for future reference. There are a number of things to consider.

Hold an internal review

It is useful to document what went well, what you would be happy to do again and what definitely did not work or could be improved. Consider also the performance of the rest of the project team. Where they good team players? Were they innovative? Did the client pay on time? Did they appreciate your contribution?, etc.

Financial performance

Analyse the income against the cost of the project. Did you achieve the level of profit anticipated at the outset of the project? Analyse the hours spent on each stage of the project; this will provide useful data for your future fee proposals.

Record the completed project

Obtain the client's permission to photograph the completed building, and use the photographs for publicity purposes. Ask your client for a statement on the building and your performance for use in publicity material. Consider any awards that may be appropriate, and prepare a project summary sheet for use in future submissions.

Archive the information

Go through all the documentation received on the project and remove any duplications. Store all the remaining documents, either electronically or in hard copy, in the office for access during the rectification period. At the end of the period, conduct a more formal review. Retain those documents that may need to be referenced during the 12- or 6-year liability period, and place them in an archive. Consider all the details, and enhance your BIM library with successful components and details.

Conducting a final inspection

Throughout the rectification period, the contractor may have attended the site to correct any defects found in the works. These should be signed off by the design team as they are completed. Once the end of the rectification period is reached, a final inspection of the works should be undertaken. It is important at this point that there are no further items of work for the contractor to complete. The signing of the Final Certificate has the effect of releasing the remaining retention money to the contractor.

Obtaining feedback on your own performance

At the end of every project, there is an opportunity to gain two distinct types of feedback.

The first is about your performance as an architect. Consider sending a questionnaire to your client, the contractor and the rest of the design team. After the completion of a number of questionnaires, you will be able to set a benchmark for your activities and your average score. By keeping good records, you will be able to demonstrate to future clients what others think of your performance. You may also wish to conduct this type of feedback questionnaire face to face with some of the team, so that you can identify those areas where improvements can be made (see Figure 5.1).

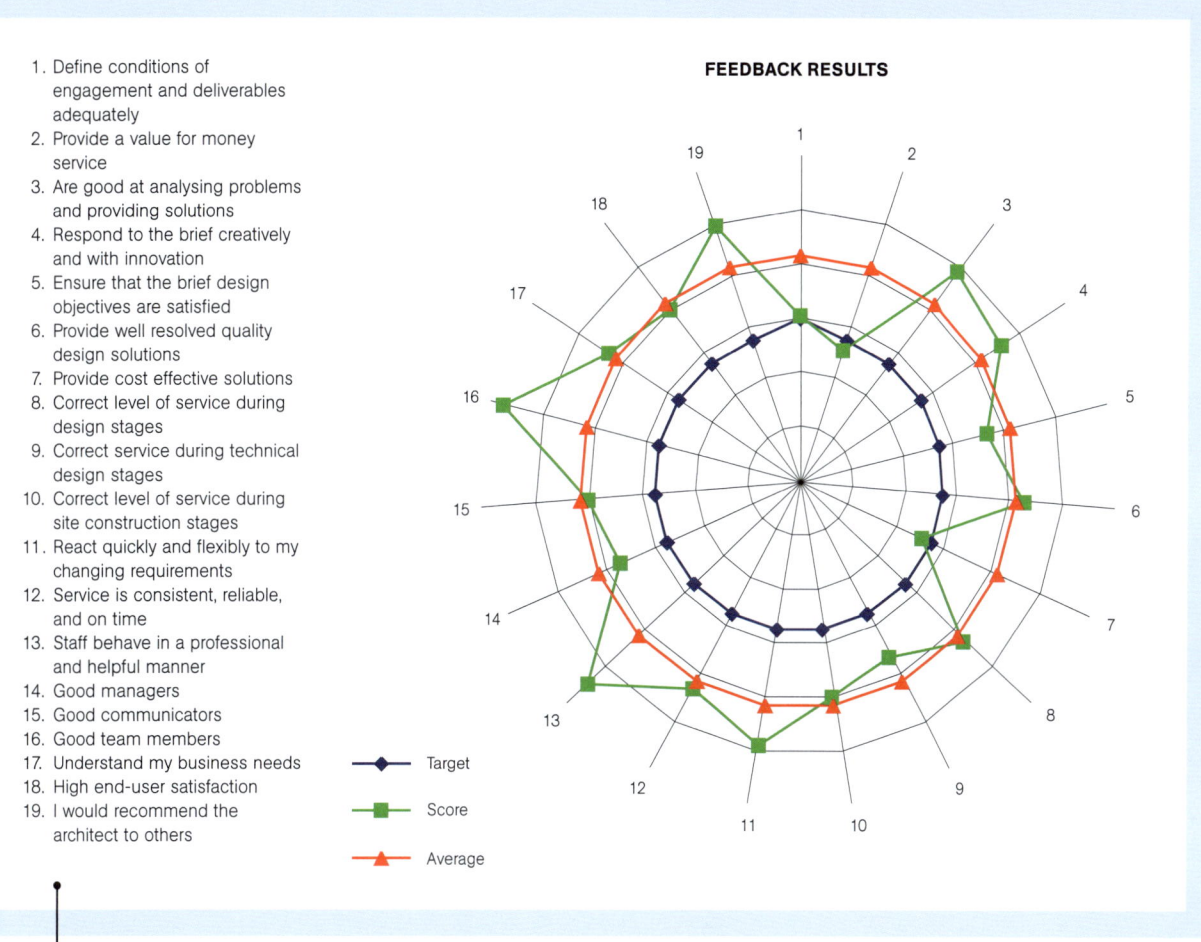

1. Define conditions of engagement and deliverables adequately
2. Provide a value for money service
3. Are good at analysing problems and providing solutions
4. Respond to the brief creatively and with innovation
5. Ensure that the brief design objectives are satisfied
6. Provide well resolved quality design solutions
7. Provide cost effective solutions
8. Correct level of service during design stages
9. Correct service during technical design stages
10. Correct level of service during site construction stages
11. React quickly and flexibly to my changing requirements
12. Service is consistent, reliable, and on time
13. Staff behave in a professional and helpful manner
14. Good managers
15. Good communicators
16. Good team members
17. Understand my business needs
18. High end-user satisfaction
19. I would recommend the architect to others

FEEDBACK RESULTS

Target
Score
Average

5.1

A simple client feedback questionnaire on an architect's performance.

The green line on the chart shows the actual scores for a project completed by a client.

• The space between the blue and red line is the target area that the firm is trying to achieve to represent a quality service.

• The architects are considered to be marginally expensive by the client and also to have provided an expensive solution. This should be examined by the architect in reference to their own database and others, such as the RIBA Annual Performance Survey.

• The architects are considered to be extremely professional and outstanding 'team players'.

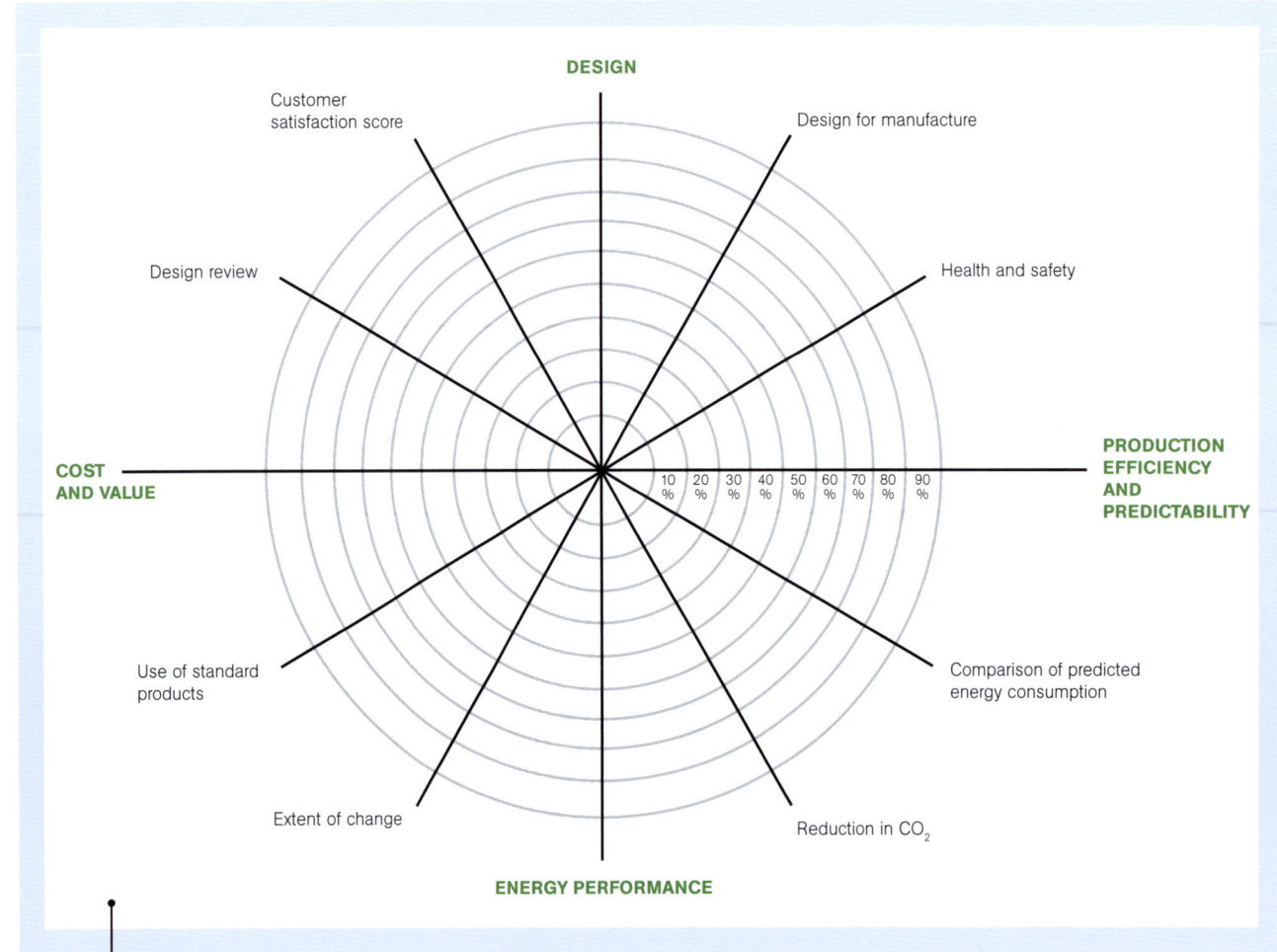

5.2
A spider diagram
recording feedback
on a building's
performance.

The second type of feedback is related more to the design solution provided by the project team. It can examine numerous different attributes of the building, depending on what is important to the client. This is a way to capture the main drivers for a project – quality, cost and value, predictability and efficiency. It is a complex matrix, and the questions need to be considered carefully in order to produce meaningful results.

SUMMARY

This chapter has described the procedure to follow when handing over a building at the end of construction. We have emphasised the importance of considering Stage 6 Handover and Close Out from the outset of the project process. We have described how this stage formally starts before Stage 5 Construction is complete, and have suggested what useful feedback can be obtained on the performance of the building and the design team. This initial feedback will be used as the foundation for a more extensive review of the building's performance throughout its life. Such additional review is covered in more detail in the first book in this series, Briefing: A Practical Guide to the RIBA Plan of Work 2013, Stages 7, 0 and 1.

SCENARIO SUMMARIES

WHAT HAS HAPPENED TO OUR PROJECTS BY THE END OF STAGE 6?

Small residential extension for a growing family

Prior to the handover meeting, a final inspection of the works is undertaken by the architect. The works are complete and to a satisfactory standard. The handover meeting takes place, and the client is guided through the operation of the equipment installed in the extension. The Practical Completion Certificate is issued, and half of the retention monies released.

The architect takes a photographic survey of the completed building for their records. The contractor removes the temporary partition separating the extension form the rest of the house allowing the familiy to move in and agrees the final account with the architect in his role as contract administrator.

After four weeks, the architect visits the client to check that everything is working as expected and to get some initial feedback on the performance of the building. It is working better than everyone expected.

Development of five new homes for a small residential developer

Due to the nature of the project there is no comprehensive Handover Strategy and the houses are handed over to the developer at practical completion together with the keys and the final meter readings of all the utilities. The developer insures the buildings until they have completed the sale of them all and passed them on to the new owners. The contractor remains on site to work systematically through the rectification list, with a view to completing the items in five weeks. The design team return to site for an additional final inspection once the works are complete.

Refurbishment of a teaching and support building for a university

The building reaches Practical Completion, and the novated design team issue a collateral warranty in favour of the university. Because the design team only had a limited involvement with the site works, their 'As-constructed' Information is issued as record drawings of their tender information to the contractor, who updates them with information from their specialist suppliers before issuing them in their Health and Safety File.

The design team agree with the client that they can return for feedback throughout the rectification period, to obtain useful information on the performance of their design. There is no direct commission for this work, so the design team must agree a retainer with the university.

New central library for a small unitary authority

The client's design team are retained for four weeks by the local authority to assist with ensuring that the building is set up correctly for use. In particular, the mechanical engineer is based on site to balance the Building Management System (BMS) and ensure that the BIM model is working in collaboration with the BMS.

The client completes the book stacking during the four-week operational readiness period, and uses this time to learn how the building is supposed to work. The architect visits site regularly to brief the staff on the proposed operation of the building.

The contractor's design team issue collateral warranties to the client for the work they have completed.

New headquarters office for high-tech internet-based company

The client accepts the building from the management contractor, and commences the move from their old offices. The design team take a full photographic record of the building at the point of Practical Completion, and issue these along with their 'As-constructed' information including drawings and models. These are subsequently used to settle a dispute over damage created by the removal company installing the furniture in the new offices.

The internet company's maintenance team hold a series of workshops with the design team in order to understand how the building works. The targets for the building's performance in use are explained, and the architect and services engineer are commissioned to undertake regular reviews of the building's performance in use. The first report is due after three months' operation, together with a rebalancing exercise on the BMS.

CHAPTER 06

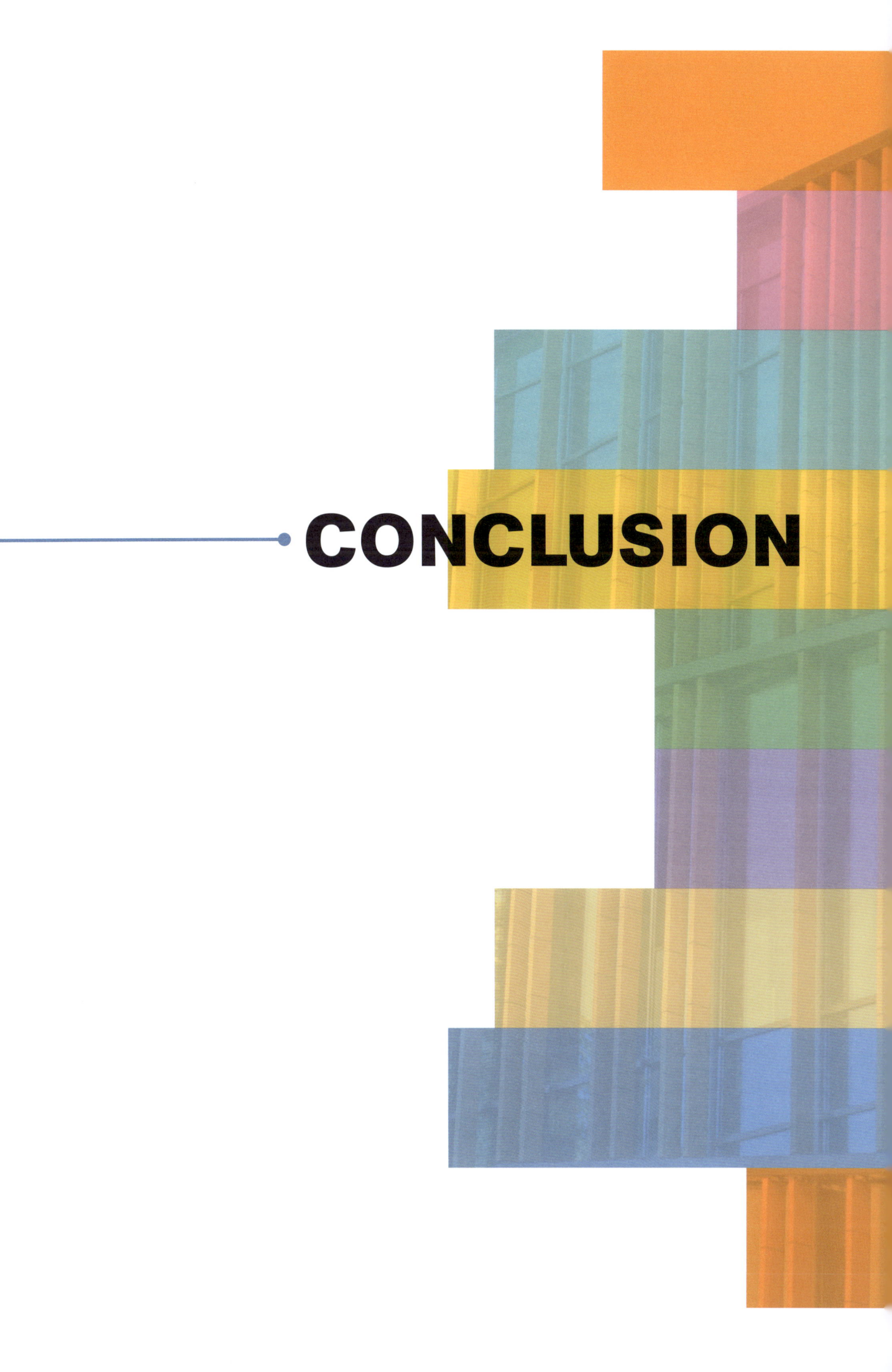

CONCLUSION

This book concentrates on the latter stages of the RIBA Plan of Work 2013, starting at Stage 4 Technical Design, through Stage 5 Construction and on to Stage 6 Handover and Close Out. It provides an insight into a number of ways in which the RIBA Plan of Work can be interpreted in order to deliver projects of all sizes and levels of complexity. There are a number of key facts, which are referenced throughout the book:

- Procurement is an essential and important part of the design process. It fundamentally influences the way in which the design team interact with those specialist subcontractors who have a design responsibility.
- The stages of a project may overlap – particularly, Stages 4 and 5. This will facilitate a quicker programme but may restrict the development of the design, as progressive fixity will be required on early packages of work.
- The RIBA Plan of Work is sequential through all its stages, even though there may be some overlap between them.
- All building design/construction professionals are working in an ever-evolving environment. Developments in construction methods, and the wider influence of BIM across the industry, will inevitably introduce an evolution in the interpretation of the RIBA Plan of Work 2013.
- The practical approach adopted in this book will provide a sound foundation for delivering any project using a design and build, management or traditional contract.
- The continuous updating of the appropriate strategies – Health and Safety, Maintenance and Operational, etc. – is important.
- The roles of the project team need to be identified on all projects. On smaller and less complex projects, a number of different roles can be undertaken by the same person.
- The responsibilities of the design team need to be understood by all the designers in detail in order to develop a fully integrated Technical Design at Stage 4.
- A collaborative approach to Technical Design and construction is essential to produce quality outcomes.
- The Information Exchanges at the end of each stage should contain the appropriate digital information to facilitate the successful start to the next stage.

Today's projects are often complex, requiring contributions from many specialist subcontractor designers in addition to the design team. The contribution of the contractor can also prove influential in the evolution of a design. To ensure that the design information is fully integrated for construction, and to encourage a collaborative approach amongst the project team throughout, the RIBA Plan of Work 2013 provides a framework for the sequential development of a project from Strategic Definition through to Handover and Close Out on a building.

WHAT HAPPENS NEXT: STAGE 7 IN USE

The RIBA Plan of Work 2013 includes an additional stage: Stage 7 In Use. This covers the life of the building after handover up to demolition. To ensure that the architectural profession continues to produce high-quality outcomes for our built environment, it is beneficial if the design team are commissioned all the way through from Stage 2 Concept Design to Stage 6 Handover and Close Out. If the designers can subsequently share in the information collected on the buildings that they have designed once they are in use, then their designs for future buildings will continue to improve.

The first book in this series will explore the role that the project team can play during Stages 7, 0 and 1 on their next project. This will include:

- How the Building Information Model can be used to maintain the building.
- How the Building Information Model can be kept up to date by the team who go on to occupy and run the building.
- How improving the measurement of a building's performance can be used for the benefit of future buildings.
- How a completed building in use can inform Stage 0 Strategic Definition on future projects.

If the designers can take this feedback and use it to inform future Stages 0 and 1 – Strategic Definition, and Preparation and Brief – then project outcomes will continue to improve. The cycle of stages can then truly become a circle of continuous improvement.

Plan of Work glossary

A number of new themes and subject matters have been included in the RIBA Plan of Work 2013. The following presents a glossary of all of the capitalised terms that are used throughout the RIBA Plan of Work 2013. Defining certain terms has been necessary to clarify the intent of a term, to provide additional insight into the purpose of certain terms and to ensure consistency in the interpretation of the RIBA Plan of Work 2013.

'AS-CONSTRUCTED' INFORMATION

Information produced at the end of a project to represent what has been constructed. This will comprise a mixture of 'as-built' information from specialist subcontractors and the 'final construction issue' from design team members. Clients may also wish to undertake 'as-built' surveys using new surveying technologies to bring a further degree of accuracy to this information.

BUILDING CONTRACT

The contract between the client and the contractor for the construction of the project. In some instances, the **Building Contract** may contain design duties for specialist subcontractors and/or design team members. On some projects, more than one **Building Contract** may be required; for example, one for shell and core works and another for furniture, fitting and equipment aspects.

BUILDING INFORMATION MODELLING (BIM)

BIM is widely used as the acronym for 'Building Information Modelling', which is commonly defined (using the Construction Project Information Committee (CPIC) definition) as: 'digital representation of physical and functional characteristics of a facility creating a shared knowledge resource for information about it and forming a reliable basis for decisions during its life cycle, from earliest conception to demolition'.

BUSINESS CASE

The **Business Case** for a project is the rationale behind the initiation of a new building project. It may consist solely of a reasoned argument. It may contain supporting information, financial appraisals or other background information. It should also highlight initial considerations for the **Project Outcomes**. In summary, it is a combination of objective and subjective considerations. The **Business Case** might be prepared in relation to, for example, appraising a number of sites or in relation to assessing a refurbishment against a new build option.

CHANGE CONTROL PROCEDURES

Procedures for controlling changes to the design and construction following the sign-off of the Stage 2 Concept Design and the **Final Project Brief**.

COMMON STANDARDS

Publicly available standards frequently used to define project and design management processes in relation to the briefing, designing, constructing, maintaining, operating and use of a building.

COMMUNICATION STRATEGY

The strategy that sets out when the project team will meet, how they will communicate effectively and the protocols for issuing information between the various parties, both informally and at Information Exchanges.

CONSTRUCTION PROGRAMME

The period in the **Project Programme** and the **Building Contract** for the construction of the project, commencing on the site mobilisation date and ending at **Practical Completion**.

CONSTRUCTION STRATEGY

A strategy that considers specific aspects of the design that may affect the buildability or logistics of constructing a project, or may affect health and safety aspects. The **Construction Strategy** comprises items such as cranage, site access and accommodation locations, reviews of the supply chain and sources of materials, and specific buildability items, such as the choice of frame (steel or concrete) or the installation of larger items of plant. On a smaller project, the strategy may be restricted to the location of site cabins and storage, and the ability to transport materials up an existing staircase.

CONTRACTOR'S PROPOSALS

Proposals presented by a contractor to the client in response to a tender that includes the **Employer's Requirements**. The **Contractor's Proposals** may match the **Employer's Requirements**, although certain aspects may be varied based on value engineered solutions and additional information may be submitted to clarify what is included in the tender. The **Contractor's Proposals** form an integral component of the **Building Contract** documentation.

CONTRACTUAL TREE

A diagram that clarifies the contractual relationship between the client and the parties undertaking the roles required on a project.

COST INFORMATION

All of the project costs, including the cost estimate and life cycle costs where required.

DESIGN PROGRAMME

A programme setting out the strategic dates in relation to the design process. It is aligned with the **Project Programme** but is strategic in its nature, due to the iterative nature of the design process, particularly in the early stages.

DESIGN QUERIES

Queries relating to the design arising from the site, typically managed using a contractor's in-house request for information (RFI) or technical query (TQ) process.

DESIGN RESPONSIBILITY MATRIX

A matrix that sets out who is responsible for designing each aspect of the project and when. This document sets out the extent of any performance specified design. The **Design Responsibility Matrix** is created at a strategic level at Stage 1 and fine-tuned in response to the Concept Design at the end of Stage 2 in order to ensure that there are no design responsibility ambiguities at Stages 3, 4 and 5.

EMPLOYER'S REQUIREMENTS

Proposals prepared by design team members. The level of detail will depend on the stage at which the tender is issued to the contractor. The **Employer's Requirements** may comprise a mixture of prescriptive elements and descriptive elements to allow the contractor a degree of flexibility in determining the **Contractor's Proposals**.

FEASIBILITY STUDIES

Studies undertaken on a given site to test the feasibility of the **Initial Project Brief** on a specific site or in a specific context and to consider how site-wide issues will be addressed.

FEEDBACK

Feedback from the project team, including the end users, following completion of a building.

FINAL PROJECT BRIEF

The **Initial Project Brief** amended so that it is aligned with the Concept Design and any briefing decisions made during Stage 2. (Both the Concept Design and **Initial Project Brief** are Information Exchanges at the end of Stage 2.)

HANDOVER STRATEGY

The strategy for handing over a building, including the requirements for phased handovers, commissioning, training of staff or other factors crucial to the successful occupation of a building. On some projects, the Building Services Research and Information Association (BSRIA) Soft Landings process is used as the basis for formulating the strategy and undertaking a **Post-occupancy Evaluation** (www.bsria.co.uk/services/design/soft-landings/).

HEALTH AND SAFETY STRATEGY

The strategy covering all aspects of health and safety on the project, outlining legislative requirements as well as other project initiatives, including the **Maintenance and Operational Strategy**.

INFORMATION EXCHANGE

The formal issue of information for review and sign-off by the client at key stages of the project. The project team may also have additional formal **Information Exchanges** as well as the many informal exchanges that occur during the iterative design process.

INITIAL PROJECT BRIEF

The brief prepared following discussions with the client to ascertain the **Project Objectives**, the client's **Business Case** and, in certain instances, in response to site **Feasibility Studies**.

MAINTENANCE AND OPERATIONAL STRATEGY

The strategy for the maintenance and operation of a building, including details of any specific plant required to replace components.

POST-OCCUPANCY EVALUATION

Evaluation undertaken post occupancy to determine whether the **Project Outcomes**, both subjective and objective, set out in the **Final Project Brief** have been achieved.

PRACTICAL COMPLETION

Practical Completion is a contractual term used in the **Building Contract** to signify the date on which a project is handed over to the client. The date triggers a number of contractual mechanisms.

PROJECT BUDGET

The client's budget for the project, which may include the construction cost as well as the cost of certain items required post completion and during the project's operational use.

PROJECT EXECUTION PLAN

The **Project Execution Plan** is produced in collaboration between the project lead and lead designer, with contributions from other designers and members of the project team. The **Project Execution Plan** sets out the processes and protocols to be used to develop the design. It is sometimes referred to as a project quality plan.

PROJECT INFORMATION

Information, including models, documents, specifications, schedules and spreadsheets, issued between parties during each stage and in formal Information Exchanges at the end of each stage.

PROJECT OBJECTIVES

The client's key objectives as set out in the **Initial Project Brief**. The document includes, where appropriate, the

employer's **Business Case, Sustainability Aspirations** or other aspects that may influence the preparation of the brief and, in turn, the Concept Design stage. For example, **Feasibility Studies** may be required in order to test the **Initial Project Brief** against a given site, allowing certain high-level briefing issues to be considered before design work commences in earnest.

PROJECT OUTCOMES

The desired outcomes for the project (for example, in the case of a hospital this might be a reduction in recovery times). The outcomes may include operational aspects and a mixture of subjective and objective criteria.

PROJECT PERFORMANCE

The performance of the project, determined using **Feedback**, including about the performance of the project team and the performance of the building against the desired **Project Outcomes**.

PROJECT PROGRAMME

The overall period for the briefing, design, construction and post-completion activities of a project.

PROJECT ROLES TABLE

A table that sets out the roles required on a project as well as defining the stages during which those roles are required and the parties responsible for carrying out the roles.

PROJECT STRATEGIES

The strategies developed in parallel with the Concept Design to support the design and, in certain instances, to respond to the **Final Project Brief** as it is concluded. These strategies typically include:

- acoustic strategy
- fire engineering strategy
- **Maintenance and Operational Strategy**
- **Sustainability Strategy**
- building control strategy
- **Technology Strategy**.

These strategies are usually prepared in outline at Stage 2 and in detail at Stage 3, with the recommendations absorbed into the Stage 4 outputs and Information Exchanges.

The strategies are not typically used for construction purposes because they may contain recommendations or information that contradict the drawn information. The intention is that they should be transferred into the various models or drawn information.

QUALITY OBJECTIVES

The objectives that set out the quality aspects of a project. The objectives may comprise both subjective and objective aspects, although subjective aspects may be subject to a design quality indicator (DQI) benchmark review during the **Feedback** period.

RESEARCH AND DEVELOPMENT

Project specific research and development responding to the **Initial Project Brief** or in response to the Concept Design as it is developed.

RISK ASSESSMENT

The **Risk Assessment** considers the various design and other risks on a project and how each risk will be managed and the party responsible for managing each risk.

SCHEDULE OF SERVICES

A list of specific services and tasks to be undertaken by a party involved in the project which is incorporated into their professional services contract.

SITE INFORMATION

Specific **Project Information** in the form of specialist surveys or reports relating to the project or site specific context.

STRATEGIC BRIEF

The brief prepared to enable the Strategic Definition of the project. Strategic considerations might include considering different sites, whether to extend, refurbish or build new and the key **Project Outcomes** as well as initial considerations for the **Project Programme** and assembling the project team.

SUSTAINABILITY ASPIRATIONS

The client's aspirations for sustainability, which may include additional objectives, measures or specific levels of performance in relation to international standards, as well as details of specific demands in relation to operational or facilities management issues.

The **Sustainability Strategy** will be prepared in response to the **Sustainability Aspirations** and will include specific additional items, such as an energy plan and ecology plan and the design life of the building, as appropriate.

SUSTAINABILITY STRATEGY

The strategy for delivering the **Sustainability Aspirations**.

TECHNOLOGY STRATEGY

The strategy established at the outset of a project that sets out technologies, including Building Information Modelling (BIM) and any supporting processes, and the specific software packages that each member of the project team will use. Any interoperability issues can then be addressed before the design phases commence.

This strategy also considers how information is to be communicated (by email, file transfer protocol (FTP) site or using a managed third party common data environment) as well as the file formats in which information will be provided. The **Project Execution Plan** records agreements made.

WORK IN PROGRESS

Work in Progress is ongoing design work that is issued between designers to facilitate the iterative coordination of each designer's output. Work issued as **Work in Progress** is signed off by the internal design processes of each designer and is checked and coordinated by the lead designer.

Index

Page numbers in italic indicate figures and in bold indicate glossary terms.